FLOW
WITH
FORCE
& FLY

Published by
Tiffany Faucette/Fighting Golf
www.fightinggolf.com

Designed by theBookDesigners
www.bookdesigners.com

Printed in USA

FG FIGHTING GOLF

FLOW WITH FORCE & FLY

TIFFANY FAUCETTE

2014 LPGA Teacher of the Year, NE

CONTENTS

ACKNOWLEDGEMENTS

A lot went into to creating *Fighting Golf*, and there are many people I need to acknowledge.

As you read through the book, you will notice pictures taken inside and outside, because you can work on your game anywhere. I'd like to thank my close friends Jim and Irene Maple for allowing me to take photos on their beautiful farm. Thank you to Mike McCartin, Alex Maravich, and Joe Martino at Title Boxing Club in Ashburn, Virginia. I work out at their gym and they allowed me to do a photo shoot using the ring and heavy bags.

There are countless PGA and LPGA professionals who extended practice privileges to me while I was traveling across the country, and I always appreciated their kindness. I'd like to thank the people who cheered for me in the gallery, and the families who opened their homes to me for housing on the Futures Tour. And a huge thank you to the LPGA, an organization I am proud to be a part of – and my appreciation grows each year.

Srixon/Cleveland Golf/XXIO is a tremendous company and has made me feel like family since they first brought me aboard as a professional staff player in 1999. I am very appreciative for all the special experiences I have had as being a part of the Srixon/Cleveland Golf/XXIO team.

Throughout this book, you will see me wearing outfits from Tail Activewear, which has been my sponsor for many years – thank you for making outfits that are so darn comfortable and good-looking!

For my dear friends and trusted brainstorming partners who helped in the conceptualization, production and proofing of this book: Carl Rabito, David Gerson, Courtney Rogers, Jack Russell, David DeWolf, Dr. Lenny Indianer, and Nancy Romps – thank you for making the creative process even more fun.

Of course, I also want to thank all my teachers and coaches during my school years that instilled a curiosity and thirst for knowledge. And a **_HUGE_** thank you to all my students … for all the fun, your friendship, and for being the true inspiration for me to write this book.

There are so many more people I would like to thank, but the Acknowledgements page would be longer than *Gone with the Wind*. One of the neat things about golf is it allows us to connect with many people and make many friends. Each person that has crossed my path during my golfing career shaped my experiences and my approach to golf, for that I thank you!

INTRODUCTION

If you think you've already heard everything about the best way to improve your game—just wait. You're about to learn that golf is a *fight*. No, not the kind of fight that gets you into trouble or jail, but a serious score to settle between you and a tiny white ball.

By reading this book and doing my drills, you'll learn how to stop fighting yourself on the course, and instead use that energy and adrenaline to deliver a blow to the ball. You'll understand how to *Flow with Force & Fly*™, which will bring your game from struggle to smooth. Gear up now to change your mindset, adjust your body, and be ready to strike on the course. Finally, it's time to *fight back*!

Golf is hard. How many times have you heard those words, or you became so frustrated with the game you wanted to quit? Probably too many to count.

Have you also wondered why so many good athletes come to the game of golf and find they are pretty bad at it? It has never made any sense to me that good athletes aren't necessarily also better golfers; by definition they have good balance, coordination, hand-eye skills, and practice habits. Does it gnaw at you that you are or used to be a good athlete, but you don't think you have come close to your potential at golf?

My goal with this book is to unleash your inner athlete by changing your perspective on the golf swing – and, ultimately the game itself, so that you are in control of your mind, body, and that little white ball.

If you don't consider yourself an athlete, don't worry. Even if you're currently prone to falling down, spilling things on yourself, or aren't used to lifting heavy objects, this book can help you develop the strength, poise, and endurance required for the game of golf.

Golf is complicated. There are hundreds of thousands of pages written about the game, numerous DVDs and instructional videos, and too many tips to count on YouTube. With so much information, how do you know what is right and what works for you? No one has enough time to test them all. **So why will this book work for you**? It will work because the concepts presented will *make sense* to you. You have made these movements before – you just didn't know how to relate them to your golf swing. Once you do, you will be able to see how one motion leads into the next.

Let me tell you a quick story about my golf experience. I started playing golf when I was 17. I had the ability to make fairly decent contact right off the bat – but golf made no sense to me whatsoever. I heard the other golfers at the club talking about swing mechanics and what they thought I should do to improve my swing. It all sounded so bizarre! However, I was new to the game – what did I know? They *must* know more than I do. Sure, I *could* hit it better, but these people in my mind were experts in the game because they had played longer and could score better. So I just agreed and tried whatever was suggested.

After my first time on the range, my dad went out and got a bunch of golf magazines and books for me to study. Again, I was completely confused. All I saw were arms and legs going everywhere, and bulging veins in the neck and arms. Each golfer seemed to be in a different position and I didn't know who to copy. Meanwhile, I was supposed to do *all* of these contortions at 100 miles per hour.

I spent most of my playing career somewhat confused about swing mechanics. I was a great competitor, had lots of grit, and was a good short game player – but **I could never truly trust my swing because I didn't *understand* the swing**. However all that changed when I changed my perspective on two simple things:

1) I stopped thinking of my swing as a "golf" swing. Instead I began to view the clubhead as a heavy weight; and
2) I thought about how to be able to fight or wield a sword at different points in my swing.

I want this book to be different than other golf books that you have read, giving you new ways to view this beautiful, one-second activity that has the potential to launch the ball great distances based on your strength and swing speed.

You will also hear that you need to have a sense of humor to play this game. I *completely* agree! I hope there are points in this book that give you a little giggle. I am very serious about punishing the ball ... but I like to goof around a bit to get there. **Golf is fun!** However, the game isn't so much fun when you are struggling to hit the ball and muttering after each swing. A large part of the fun in golf is hitting it solidly and watching the ball fly! You will learn how to do that as you progress through this book.

You should be able to glide through your swing with balance and power. Ideally you should be able to ***Flow with Force and Fly!*™ Let's begin the journey of making you the athlete you know you are, with a golf club in your hands.**

THE STRUGGLE...TO THE MEANING

Sometimes in life you are just lucky, and I have been lucky to have the right people come into my life at the right time. It started at birth when I met my parents. There are no words for how much they have done for me.

My mom always pushed me and set the bar exceptionally high. I will never forget the words she said to me during a Match Play amateur event, when I had my opponent seven down with eight holes to play. I got too aggressive with a birdie putt and ended up losing the hole. Now I was six up with seven holes to play. My mom walked over to me, looked me in the eyes with complete intensity, and said, "You gave her life. *Now go kill her!*" I just started laughing. I said, "You do know we are playing *golf*, right?"

My mom didn't play golf, but she had been the captain of her college basketball team. The likelihood of me losing that match was almost nonexistent, but she was worried I was letting the momentum shift. (I did win the match on the next hole.)

We tease Mom to this day about that line. What it showed to me is what a fighter she is, and how you need to compete on *every* shot, at *every* second, and never take anything for granted.

My dad introduced me to the game and ended up caddying for me for most of my competitive career. He had played quarterback in college and some professional football in his day, winning the championship with the Hartford Knights in the Atlantic Coast Conference League (similar to the USFL) and playing on farm teams for the Dallas Cowboys and New York Giants. He taught me how to train and practice. He was the best at analyzing things and setting up strategies.

As a competitive golfer, I played in all the major USGA events as an amateur and on every major professional women's tour at the time. Primarily I played on the Futures Tour, but also spent a couple seasons on the European Tour, Canadian Tour, Asian Tour, and others. I played a handful of LPGA events including two majors: the U.S. Open and the McDonald's Championship. And if there were some sort of mini-tour event anywhere, I teed up in it. The goal of playing all those tournaments is to sharpen your game enough to advance through Q-School. (To attain playing privileges on the LPGA Tour, or the PGA Tour for that matter, you have to advance through a series of tournaments nicknamed "Q-school," short for Qualifying School.) **As any aspiring golfer knows, Q-School comes but once a year, and dictates the next twelve months of your life.**

I had practiced like a fiend, and I was ready. As per tradition at the time, the first stage of Q-School was in Palm Desert, California. To make a long story short, I missed advancing to final stage of Q-School by one shot, and I was devastated. I can still see the look in my dad's face; he was so disappointed too. He had caddied and worked his tail off for me, and we just *barely* missed. We got in the car and went to lunch at the casino down the road; it had a huge buffet, and I guess my dad thought I needed the comfort of the dessert bar.

Then I looked up at my dad and said, "I'm done."

"But you have barely eaten," he answered.

I said, "No, Dad, I am done with golf. I am quitting."

He looked at me with sad eyes and said it is was my decision. He knew how long and hard I had been trying. It was one of the worst emotional days of my life; I still can't think about it without being right back at that table.

We sat quietly until my dad said, "I know you want to quit – but you are too good and have worked too hard. Will you make me a deal?"

He said to take two weeks off. "Then I want you to go see a golf instructor named Carl Rabito," Dad continued. "After you go and work with him, you can decide if you want to quit."

I looked at my dad like he was nuts – but he was my dad. If this was what he needed in order to know we had exhausted *every* way to succeed, I would do it.

The next couple of weeks were rough; I didn't know what I was going to do. But each day I was more sure I was going to switch gears and find an entirely different career. I had too much golf scar tissue and was ready for something new.

But being the good daughter I am, I drove to Clermont, Florida, and met Carl Rabito. On the way there I fully expected to shake Carl's hand and hit a few balls. I expected him to tell me about the same swing flaws that I already knew I had, and countless other teachers had tried to help me fix. Then I would thank him for the lesson and then be officially done with game.

What happened the next two hours changed my life. Carl taught me more in two hours than I had learned in golf up to that point. He showed me how things were dictated by my bone structure. His philosophy is Structure Governs Function™ – meaning the way something is designed dictates how it can move or function. He showed me how I needed to set my bones up so I could function for golf. It was a way at looking at golf from a whole new perspective for me. I liked school and learning, and I love absolutes. Carl set my brain on fire; for the first time in years I was as energized about golf as I ever had been.

Carl was also tough, like my mom. He taught me a mindset that serves me well to this day. And he showed me ways to use force and leverage of my body in the golf swing that were just amazing. The moves were freeing and powerful to execute. My ball striking got so much better after working with Carl that there isn't a day that goes by that I don't wish I had met him when I first started playing golf.

The more time I spent with Carl, the more I became completely immersed in study of the human body and instruction of the game. I competed for another year or two, made a bunch of cuts, and qualified for the US Open – but I was tired of traveling, and the expense of playing on tours just below the LPGA was becoming too much.

I asked Carl if he would mentor me and help me become an elite instructor like he is. He did, and I am honored to say that Carl is still the one I turn to if I have a question. He is a true friend, and I have the utmost respect for him and all that he has done to help me.

It didn't make any sense to me at the time, but all those crushing disappointments during my playing career led me to write this book. There just *had* to be a better way … a better way to learn the game, a better way to communicate the game, and a better way to feel confident about your swing so it holds up under pressure. This may sound weird, but I have always felt like I was going to make an impact on the game. I initially thought I was going to do it as a player on the LPGA Tour; I had no idea my real calling was as a teacher, to make the game enjoyable for *anyone* who wants to pick up a club and punish that little white ball.

I get tremendous joy out of working with my students. I love showing them how they can move easier and hit farther just by leveraging their body. Each day on the range it is fun for me. I like showing people how to connect the dots; teaching them to **Flow with Force & Fly**! And it never gets old when they turn back at me with a beaming smile after they crush a shot.

All this backstory brings me to this book.

For years, my students would ask me if I had a book that they could refer to. I would say,

"No. If I gave you the book, I wouldn't get to see you as much." As time went by, "the book" became a joke. When a student would ask a question, I would say something like, "Chapter 4 of my book explains how you do that!" Once I stopped joking about "the book" and began writing it, I decided to go a step further, creating training aids and instructional videos.

You see, learning goes in stages. First you need to *understand*; the book and videos give a golfer knowledge of how the body and club work together through the swing. The next part of learning involves *experiencing*; this is where training aids come in. Countless golfers put in the practice time but don't get the results they want because they haven't developed proper body awareness and a feedback system.

After giving thousands upon thousands of lessons, I saw for myself exactly what golfers need to put the pieces together to figure out their own swing. So I built it myself! As it turns out, I built what *I* needed when I was competing. (The training aids I am referring to went for prototyping at the same time this book went to print. So they aren't available yet.) I used a bunch of training aids back in my playing days, but none of them did exactly what I needed and some needed assembly, which isn't my thing. Better yet, what I built works for golfers of all levels. Why? Because the bone structure for all humans is basically the same, and the physics of golf doesn't change whether you're a novice or a pro. I tell you all this because I am obsessed with helping people get better at golf in any way I can.

To wrap up the background of Fighting Golf, I'd like to explain my tagline to you: *Flow with Force and Fly*! These three action words sum up the way I approach every swing and every lesson.

- *Flow* is your relationship with the club: the fluid motion comes from the body and club working in balance with each other.
- *Force* is how you leverage your body to transfer energy right to the ball.
- And *Fly* is the end product of Flow and Force – the flight of the ball that takes your breath away when it's done right.

Keep *Flow with Force and Fly* in mind as you read the tips in the book, during drills, and *every* time you're Fighting Golf. As you gain greater understanding of your body mechanics, these concepts will make complete sense to you.

I look forward to being your trusty mentor for improvement. I hope I can help you see your golf swing from a new perspective. And I hope I can infuse the same enthusiasm in you as Carl Rabito did in me.

WHY FIGHTING GOLF?

Fighting is about hitting someone, and golf is about hitting some*thing*.

Fighting is pretty easy to understand, so I hope thinking about golf as fighting will help you better understand your golf swing. In reality, **golf is just a combination of fighting, chopping, and throwing** motions. You are capable of doing *all* those things, which is why I believe *anyone* has the capability to become a more than decent golfer.

Question: Have you ever wondered who created the game of golf?
Take a second, and think about the answer to the question above. The answer may surprise – and inspire – you.

While no one knows for sure, most historians believe that shepherds in Scotland started the game back in the 1400s. Do you think that shepherds would have created a game that you need a PhD to play? What did these people do? They chopped wood, cut down trees, lifted heavy objects, and chased sheep – so when they created the game of golf, they were having *fun*. They were hitting a ball with a stick – and they were moving in familiar ways.

So here is the **first lesson: You are hitting a ball with a stick** – and that stick is important. From now on, you should always consider the clubhead to be nothing more than a *very heavy weight.*

Keep this tucked in the back of head: You are going to learn how to **"Wield the Weight."** And you'll learn that **The Weight Always Wins!™**

CONCEPTS TO UNDERSTAND
BEFORE WORKING ON YOUR SWING

Hitting good golf shots is a combination of many components; however, there are two crucial pieces of your golf swing puzzle that you need to understand before you start hitting balls.

1) You need to understand the collision.
2) Your golf equipment needs to fit you.

UNDERSTANDING THE COLLISION
Take a moment and answer this question in your head: "How does the ball get in the air?" Let's see here ... you hit it." Yes, but go deeper. How *exactly* does the clubhead

strike the ball? Does the clubhead have to get *under* the ball? Does it hit the *side* of the ball/the equator? Or does it hit just *above* the equator?

If you answered "get under the golf ball," there's no doubt in my mind that you are making a swing motion that causes you to release the clubhead early and leave weight on your back foot as you attempt to finish your swing. But don't feel bad! That's the most common answer I get when I ask the question of how the ball gets in the air.

When I first started playing golf, I thought you had to get the clubhead under the ball. How else was it going to get in the air? It made sense to me that the ball would get "up" if you slid the clubhead under the ball. Also, I was told I had to stay behind the ball with straight arms, so with that thought template working in my subconscious, getting under the ball made sense. Unfortunately, the physics of golf was working against me.

If you answered that the ball gets in the air by hitting just above the equator of the ball, you are correct (and it tells me you are a student of the game!). Hitting slightly *above* the equator makes perfect sense as I'm writing this, but I totally understand it's hard to think about when you're actually executing a golf shot. Let's make it simpler.

A ball gets in the air when the *entire golf ball* is hit with the face of the golf club with speed. The best shots happen when your hands are slightly closer to the target than the clubhead at impact. Bottom-line: you want to hit the ball from the side in a *downward* manner.

Keep in mind the golf club is a big piece of metal, and if it collides into the ball with enough speed it will move. It may even get in the air; it just won't maximize what you are capable of.

The next time you go to hit a golf ball, think about *squishing* it. For that ideal shot with good trajectory, the weight of the club collides with ball in such a manner in which the ball gets squished between the turf and the clubhead. The result of this is the ball has to roll up the face of the golf club. This is how backspin is created, which helps with the lift/launch of the ball.

In order to squish the ball, the shaft has to be on a slight forward lean at impact. When this happens you will most likely make contact where the entire golf ball makes contact with the face of the golf club. When you hit the *entire* ball, you get the best lift and best shots!

If the golf club is leaning away from the target at impact, you most likely will hit the ball with the "leading edge" of the golf club; while the ball may get in the air, it normally comes off "thin" or with a lower trajectory.

To recap: The weight of the clubhead falls on the ball, and the loft of the club is what propels the ball into the air. Simply understanding how to properly compress the ball will help your body motion. You will move differently if you are trying to return the club on a shaft lean *toward* the target vs. away from the target at impact.

▶▶▶▶▶▶ **TIFFBIT**   I have always *hated* the term "hit down on it," because when I first started playing it sounded like I needed to hit directly on top of the ball and drive it into the ground.

My dad and I used to have fights about this on the driving range because I have a very literal mind. The words he was saying to me weren't convincing me to perform the action he wanted.

Quick funny story: One day my father was frustrated with me because I kept hitting thin shots. He kept saying: "Stop flipping! You have to hit *down* on the ball! I don't care what you do, but hit down on this next ball!" (He didn't say it *quite* that nicely.) Since I am stubborn, I looked up at him and said, "Okay." I started my swing, made a chopping motion, and hit exactly on top of the ball, like I was going to chop it in two. The ball careened off in weird way and almost killed another golfer on the range. Needless to say, that was the end of the practice session.

I look back at those times now and laugh. Even after that event, it still took me quite some time to understand what made the ball perform. I couldn't figure out how some of the body motions I was being asked to do would allow me to do anything but try and slide the club under the golf ball.

I now know the best results come from striking the ball from the side in a downward manner.

I hope the rest of this book will provide some clarity for you. Unfortunately, much of the traditional terminology in golf isn't the best verbiage to explain the desired motions. Words create images ... and hopefully movements. After giving thousands upon thousands of lessons, I now consider myself a bit of a "golf translator." The game really isn't *that* hard if the right words and concepts are used. However, the game is *impossible* if you don't understand a term, or the message conveyed causes you to do something undesirable.

Earlier I mentioned you need to understand two things before working on your swing: the collision, and how important it is to have clubs that fit *you*. In order to have clubs that fit you, you need to have a good balanced posture. So I am going to start with information on balance and posture before talking about golf clubs. I promise I will circle back to the golf club information.

Let's jump right in and get you ready to move and ready to swing. It all starts with you having a *dynamically balanced posture* position.

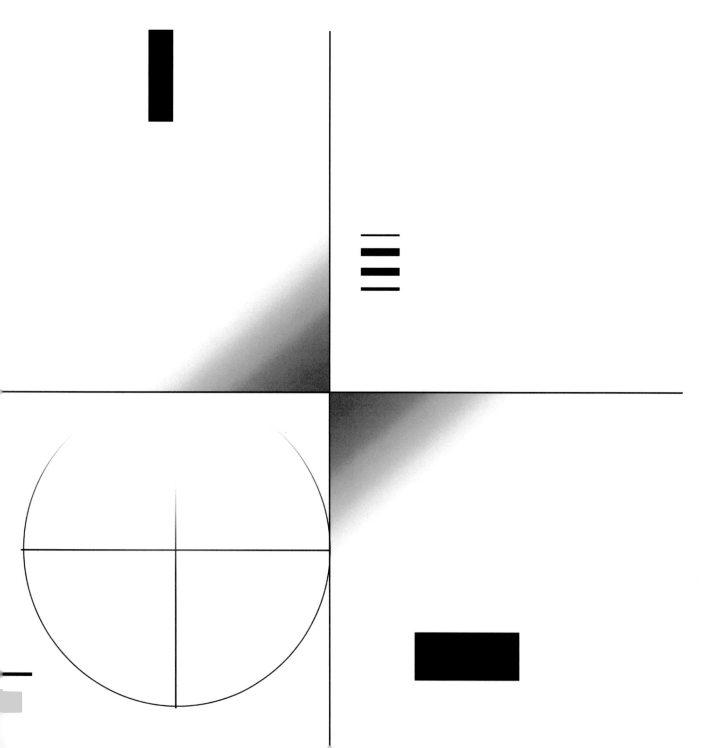

BALANCE

Balance is important in golf. You hear this buzzword all the time. It is critically important to set up in a balanced position because your body is always seeking balance. If your setup position is out of balance, you will start making adjustments during your swing in an attempt to get back in balance. The goal is to start in balance and swing in balance. Bottom line, you can swing more powerfully and without compensation if you are in balance.

So what is balance? By definition, according to Oxford Dictionary, **balance** is an even distribution of weight enabling someone, or something, to remain upright and steady; synonyms include stability, equilibrium, and steadiness.

In golf, you're always doing multiple things at once. The swing requires lots of coordination, much like patting your head and rubbing your stomach while jumping on one foot and turning around.

In golf, you are balancing two things at once: your body in tandem with the golf club. If the club gets out of balance during the swing, it forces your body out of position in an attempt to get the club back in balance, to deliver the blow on to the golf ball.

In order to master your balance, you need to control your center of gravity, your sternum, and your head. In order to control it, you need to know where your center of gravity is located. (I'm presuming you already know where your head and sternum are located!)

Question: Where is your center of gravity in your body?
Answer: Your center of gravity is two inches below your belly button. You want to keep your center of gravity between your feet and on top of your arches at your address position. As this chapter progresses, we will talk more about your center of gravity.

Question: Where should the weight be in your feet at address?
Answer: Evenly distributed on your feet – you want to feel the weight distributed 50/50 from front to back and left to right.

Go back to the definition of balance – balance is evenly distributed so you don't want the majority of your weight in your toes at address, because by definition you are out of balance. Conversely, you don't want too much weight in the heels, because again you will be starting out of balance and will need to make a maneuver once you start moving to regain balance.

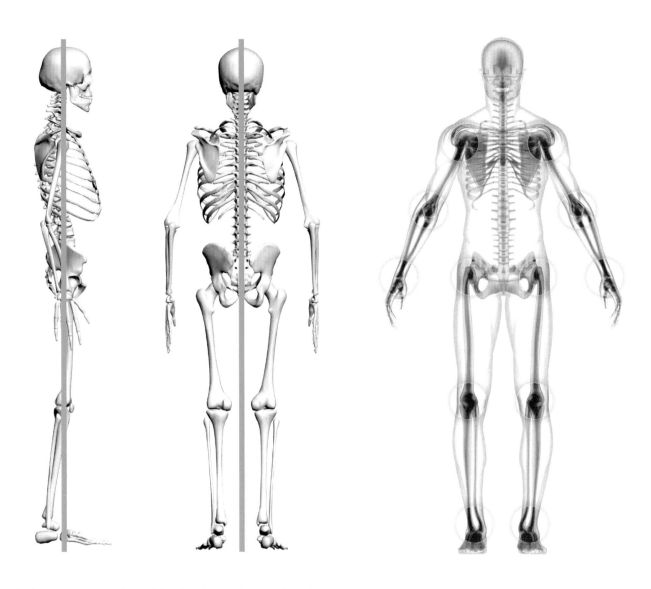

Take a moment and look at each photo above.

The skeleton on the right illustrates you are a spine with six sets of joints: shoulders, elbows, wrists, hips, knees, and ankles. Positioning and movement of these joints are vital in the golf swing.

You know how to command your body. And most of the time moving is simple for you. You move through the day, not giving a moment's thought on how to do something. Say you drop a pen on the ground – you don't think about how to get it, you just *get* it. Likewise, you don't think about how you have to bend at your hip joints to get into your car – you just *do* it. All day long you instinctively know how to command your upper body, lower body, and extremities to do whatever you want.

The problem is you are about to make a golf swing – and golf swings make no sense! And for many people, once they bend over at their hips, their brains shut off ... just kidding!

Take a look at the skeletons on the left of page 12. The one on the right has a line drawn through the midline of the body. Notice on the left skeleton how the line goes through the arches of the feet. That is where you want to have your balance point in your feet at address. And remember, your center of gravity in your body is two inches below your belly button.

GOLF CLUB BALANCE POINTS
DURING THE SWING

The balance point of a golf club is defined as the point where a shaft's weight is evenly distributed in both directions when rested on a single point. Most golfers understand that concept when measuring a club during a fitting, but very few think about where the club is balanced *during* the swing.

There are four balance points during the golf swing for the golf club. One balance point is at the top of the backswing. The other balance points occur when the club is parallel to the ground; **the club is parallel to the ground three times during the golf swing**.

The golf club is in balance, from the down-the-line view, when the club is parallel to the ground and the target line at the same time. At the same time, your arms would be in a position where they could hold a heavy weight the longest.

Take a golf club, grip it, and hinge the club up right in front of you. The clubhead will feel light because it is directly above, or in line with, your hands.

With your hands still in a hinged position and the clubhead directly above your hands, allow the club to tilt to one side. You will notice the clubhead will start to feel heavier.

When a golf club is out of position, it gets heavier in motion and it starts to affect your body motion. If the club starts to get out of position, you *have* to do something to try and get back in position.

For the rest of this book, the words **position** and **balance** are synonymous. If you are in position, then you will be balanced, and vice-versa.

Throughout this book you will hear me say, "**Take care of the straight lines, and the curves will take care of themselves.**" The straight lines are the balance points for the shaft when it is parallel to the ground. During the swing, if you hit the three straight lInes where the club is balanced, almost everything else will fall into place.

BALANCE POINTS FOR THE GOLF CLUB

BALANCE POINT 1 - BACKSWING
Face-on View: When the club shaft is parallel to the ground in the backswing.
Down-the-Line View: When the club shaft is parallel to the target line with the clubhead in line with the golfer's hands.
(Will be discussed more during Position 1)

BALANCE POINT 2 - DOWNSWING
Face-on View: When the club shaft is parallel to the ground in the downswing.
Down-the-Line View: When the club shaft is parallel to the target line with the clubhead in line with the golfer's hands.
(Will be discussed more in Position 3)

BALANCE POINT 3 - FORWARD SWING
Face-on View: When the club shaft is parallel to the ground in the forward swing.
Down-the-Line View: When the club shaft is parallel to the target line with the clubhead in line with the golfer's hands.
(Will be discussed more in Position 5)

There is one more balance point for the club at the top of the swing, but for the purposes of this book we will focus on the three balance points when the club is parallel to the ground. Now that you understand where your center of gravity is, and the importance of the balance points of the golf club, we will start to talk about your body positioning and the Power Platform. We will also get more into how you have to maneuver your head, sternum, and center of gravity in harmony throughout the swing.

All of this may seem hard, but it isn't – you do it fairly naturally in other sports where you have to react. As we go through the drills, you will see how to relate your golf swing to other sports, and how to position your body for good ball striking.
Keep in mind that **you must be set up properly to be able to balance your body and club in tandem throughout the swing.**

KNOW YOUR BONES

Take a minute and look at all the skeletons in this chapter. You can just tell something is off in the golf skeletons, on page 17. However, far too many golfers either setup or swing like those golf skeletons. I see golfers like this on the driving range every day. What has them in these positions is based on what they interpreted from the golf information they had received so far.

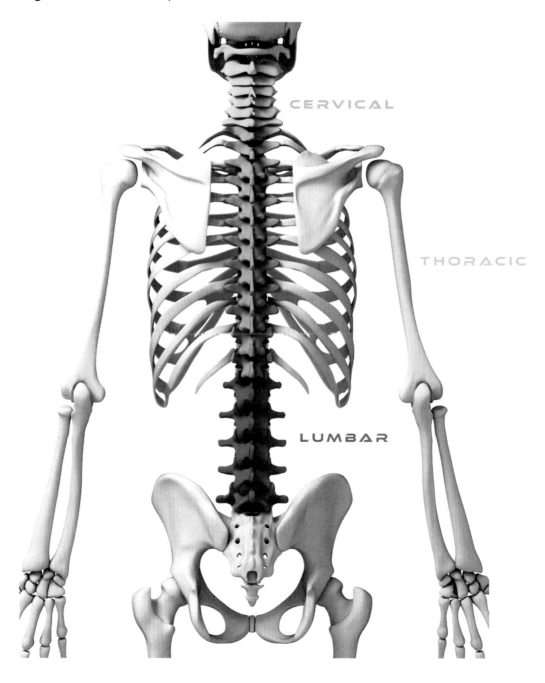

CERVICAL

THORACIC

LUMBAR

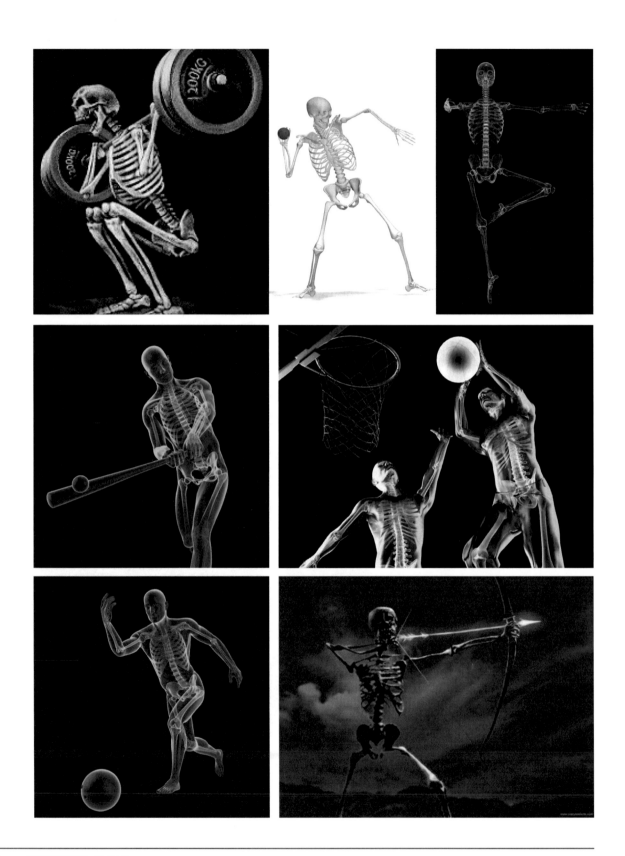

Truly, the reason I think most good athletes aren't as good at golf, as you would think they would be, is because much of the golf information out there forces a person into a "non-athletic" or "non-instinctive" motion. If someone told me to throw a ball, I would keep my head down, my butt out, and my arm straight; I would look at that person like they were crazy. But many people have been told to do all of the above in order to hit a golf ball ... and they just say, "Okay." Most golfers don't know they are supposed to do something *better*. I believe that is where the term "hit and hope" came from. They *know* they are in a weird position ... but golf is weird, right? So this crazy positioning must be correct, right? WRONG!

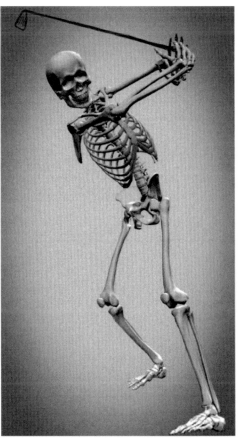

I would love for that archer skeleton (previous page, bottom right) to take out those two dreadful golf skeletons and put them out of their poor shot-making misery!

I want to make you feel so good about your swing that you can feel it *in your bones*. When your bones are set up properly and you are moving without pain, your subconscious knows the move is "good." Many golfers have fragile confidence levels. Their subconscious knows that it is going to be difficult to make good contact repeatedly if they are set up in a way that requires extra compensation for a solid strike.

The last thing you want to do is address the ball in such a manner that your own bones block you during the swing. You should *glide*, not grind, through your swing.

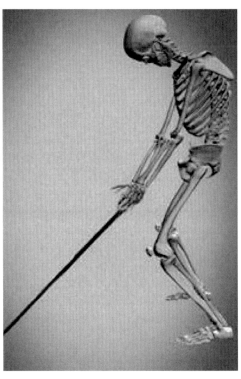

Keep going back to the posture and grip portions of this book so we can get your bones positioned and moving properly. Let's go create a superior skeleton for your swing!

GOLF INJURIES – CREATED BY SELF-INFLICTED BODY BLOWS

Everyone understands the concept of body blows in boxing.

bod·y blow: Noun; A heavy punch to the body. A severe disappointment or crushing setback. (Oxford Dictionary)

In boxing, you want to *deliver* body blows – not take any yourself. Weirdly enough, most golfers are beating themselves up when they swing with self-induced body blows.

If you follow golf at all, or just see the headlines in the news, you know about Tiger Woods' surgeries. You also know that golfers get lots of injuries.

Golf is not a *contact* sport like football and today's modern basketball. So why are all these golfers getting injured? Simply put, they are hitting themselves. No, not *literally* hitting themselves; the way they are swinging is causing trauma to the body, so they may as well have hit themselves.

Most golfers are giving themselves self-induced body blows with each swing, by either forcing themselves past a natural range of motion in a joint, or by having their bones grind on one another during the swinging motion.

Let's examine some things I regularly hear a new student say, as a cue for their golf swing.

EXAMPLE 1:
New Student: "I know I have made a good backswing when my front shoulder hits my chin."
Me: "Why do you want to hit yourself? Name me one other time in anything you do where you would like your shoulder to touch your chin.

The student thinks for a while, laughs, and says, "I can't."

In everyday life, our shoulders live far away from our face, and we want that during our golf swing too. It allows our bones and muscles to stay where they normally live throughout the swing, without getting crushed or twisted.

And for the ladies out there: If you have been practicing having your shoulder hit your chin on the backswing, you probably have a ton of makeup on the sleeve of your front arm – better mechanics can keep your clothes clean *and* make your body feel better too!

EXAMPLE 2:
New Student: "I want to start my downswing with my hips."
Me: "When you throw a punch do you think about your hips?"

For most golfers, if they start their downswing too quickly with their hips, their torso falls back and away from the target. When a golfer rotates their lower body as their upper body is falling back, they are creating trauma and grinding the bones of the lower back.

Again this results in dull and excessive pain, depending on how often you hit balls and how much speed you create when hitting those balls.

DR. DIVOT'S GUIDE TO GOLF INJURIES
BOOK EXCERPT (LARRY FOSTER, MD., F.A.A.O.S 2004)

"Women golfers (amateur and pro) run the same overall high risk of injury as the men (about an 80 percent injury rate for professionals and about 60 percent for the amateurs, regardless of gender). The left (lead) side is most at risk for all golfers, regardless of their skill level or gender.

The overall pattern of distribution of injuries by body part is similar for females and males. One exception to the trend, however, is the disproportionately high rate of back injuries seen among men as compared with women. This is true for both professionals and amateur golfers. Conversely, female golfers (amateur and pro) are more likely to sustain injuries to the upper limb (elbow, wrist, and hand) than male golfers."

My take: These findings are not surprising to me. Injuries are so common in golf now that rotoworld.com has an Injury List for the PGA Tour, just like the NFL has an injured reserve list.

It also doesn't surprise me that the lead side of the body has the majority of the injuries. This is because our lead hand and arm take the brunt of the vibration if the clubhead is out of position at impact. If the clubhead hits the ground before the ball, this will send vibration/trauma through the wrists and elbows. If a golfer misses impact by letting the clubhead pass the hands prior to impact, the left wrist will be in a hinged or "flipped" position jamming some of small wrists bones in the front wrist. We also move into our lead side with the weight transfer. If the weight transfer isn't done properly it can add extra stress to the hip, knees, and ankles.

Prevention is a key word these days. **The only way I can help you prevent these injuries is by helping you CREATE a completely fluid motion!** For some of you, it might be a completely new motion.

Bottom line: I want to get you in positions that you would get into to backhand or hit something if you didn't have a club in your hand. I need to get you in some fighting positions *with* a golf club in your hands!

PAINFUL PARTS - WHICH PARTS HURT ON YOU?

Take a look at the pictures below. You can see how the body is positioned during that particular golf swing, and which part of your body would end up with some pain. I am just going to show a position that would cause pain, and highlight the area that gets the most trauma. Remember your bones and joints are connected throughout your body – the jingle "Head, Shoulders, Knees and Toes" comes to mind. Sometime the trauma caused in the body is referred to another part of the body.

LOWER BACK PAIN – Starting the downswing with the hips in such a manner where the upper body falls back.

NECK PAIN – Keeping head down after impact. You can see the strain in the neck. It looks like the vein wants to pop out of his body.

SHOULDER PAIN – Lifting the arms high in the sky in the backswing, you can see the strain in the muscles around the front shoulder.

ELBOW PAIN – The pointing part of the elbow is out of position and will add strain during the swing. Besides, it looks weird; we rarely show the inside part of our elbow.

HAND/WRIST PAIN – the hands are positioned where the wrists can't effectively hinge.

(Addressed more in the Grip Chapter)

KNEE PAIN – Either bracing them at address, or excessively "popping/posting" them on the follow through.

(Addressed more in the Posture Section)

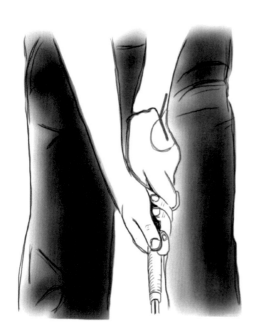

ANKLE PAIN – Rolling to the outside edge of the foot on the backswing or at the finish. You don't want to finish on the outside edge of the foot, like in the picture. This puts too much stress on the ankle.

COMMON SENSE - More pictures that just look painful. If you are new to the game, you might not know what to do...but you know what *not* to do. Trust yourself, and don't allow yourself to get all contorted.

Look at this picture of Happy Gilmore; he was onto something. You will be able to relate more to this picture in our discussion of Position 2 later in the book. He is *almost* in the position I would like for you to be at the top of your backswing.

Notice a few things – a preface of what's to come:
He is leaning away from the target at the top of the backswing.
He is looking at the golf ball.
His nose is actually pointed in front of the golf ball.
His hands are not over his head.
His back hip is lower than his front hip.
His back arm is higher than front arm.
His legs are strong and flexed.

I included a picture resembling Happy Gilmore because the position he is in does not look painful or weird. It is a believable position you could imagine how to mimic. Now flip back one page and look at the pictures again – they all look painful, and a little weird. Instinctively, you know mimicking those positions might not be a good idea. **Trust your eyes and your gut – if it looks weird, it _is_ weird.**

Bottom line: There are three main ways to hurt yourself when you play:

1) Having bone grind on bone though a movement
2) Trying to rotate your spine through a side crunch
3) Stretching your bones out of a socket will strain or tear the muscles (hence the reason for rotator cuff and labrum tears, etc.)

Snap, Crackle, Pop is great for cereal … but not our bodies. None of us like it when we hear our bodies go Snap, Crackle, Pop!

In order to stop the Snap, Crackle, Pop, golfers have to eliminate the Grind, Crunch, and Strain movements during the swing. You should be able to _glide,_ not grind, through your swing.

As you read through this book and master the posture, grip, and six striking positions, you will be able to *"Glide and Go!"* which creates **Flow, Force, and Fly!**

And remember... **LOOK NORMAL AND SWING POWERFUL!**

INSIGHTS I am constantly asking my students questions. One day I decided to send out questionnaire to see what they were thinking about in regard to golf: their swings, frustrations, successes, and learning lightbulbs. During each part of the book, I will share some of their feedback. As a golfer reading this book, you are on a quest to get better, so you may relate to their train of thought. The question I sent out was:

What do you consider to be the most important part of the swing?

▶▶▶▶▶ **STUDENT THOUGHTS**

Daniel Hernandez is a scratch handicap and Purple Heart Recipient. In 2015 he advanced to the final stage of U.S. Open Qualifying — the only Purple Heart recipient to do so.

"The most important things in my golf swing are setup and tempo. If I have a good setup that is fundamental, then I will have fewer adjustments to make in my swing. Second, if my tempo taking the club back is good, my club goes back on plane and I can make a smooth transition into the downswing."

Steve Niezgoda is a golfer dedicated to figuring out this crazy game. He came to me shooting just over 100; now he regularly shoots low 80s (he even broke 80!) and has learned to chip in.

"I remember reading how the pros primarily focus on proper setup, alignment, and grip. These topics are such an eye roll if you can't even hit the ball. I've found that, like most disciplines, fundamentals become more important and relevant as skill level improves. My current belief is that I have reached a level of proficiency that, if my setup and takeaway are correct, there is a very high likelihood I will make a good swing."

"You'd think I'd be able to get into a solid address position without thinking, considering the tens of thousands of swings I've made in my lifetime. The truth is that it's as easy to fall into bad habits here as it is in any other part of your swing. So I work on my address every time I practice."

—Rory McIlroy, 4-time major championship winner
and current world-ranked number-one player

"If you set up correctly, there's a good chance you'll hit a reasonable shot, even if you make a mediocre swing. If you set up to the ball poorly, you'll hit a lousy shot even if you make the greatest swing in the world."

—Jack Nicklaus, 18-time major championship winner

"I'm paying attention to all the little things. My grip. My posture. My alignment. I felt like I was getting loose and sloppy with those things. Posture is the most important one. I have to keep checking that I'm not getting too hunched over with a rounded back."

—Adam Scott, 2013 Masters Champion

▶▶▶▶▶▶ TIFFBIT   THINKING IS RECOMMENDED

Golfers come to me all the time telling me that they are thinking too much. There is no problem with thinking if you are thinking the proper things. These golfers are having trouble because their picture of their swing mechanics isn't clear. Whenever you learn something new, you must think … period. When reading this book, allow yourself to think. I liken learning a new movement pattern in golf to swimming through Jell-O. You can do it, but it feels weird and slows you down. The more you perform the new motion pattern, the more the Jell-O turns back into water and your speed returns enhanced. Let's take the journey of educating your conscious so you can perform running off your subconscious … that is where the magic happens!

POWER PLATFORM
...POSTURE

Your body is your ultimate tool in golf – and, of course, in life! How you position *you* – your tool – determines how you can move, and ultimately how you use your body force.

Golf demands a complex set of body movements in a short period of time. Your posture must be balanced and positioned so that you can perform with consistency. In order to become the best player you can be, with the least amount of restriction in your swing, you must understand **the importance of your posture – a.k.a., the Power Platform™**.

It is difficult to get fired up to practice on your posture. Therefore, in my mind I changed the term "posture" to the Power Platform. I used the word *power* because your posture dictates how you can move and the resulting power you can generate. And I chose the word *platform* because people perform on stages and platforms. Platforms have to be balanced and sturdy so that a person has the chance to perform. Besides – it is more fun to say I have a solid Power Platform than to say I have good posture.

Always remember, you are a spine with six main sets of joints. Throughout this chapter I will explain how you position your joints and bones so that you can perform your best. The whole reason a golfer assumes the Power Platform is so that he or she can swing in balance. When you swing in balance, you can swing faster and your swing is more repeatable.

Please read the upcoming chapter – how to get into the Power Platform and the positioning of the body – *more than once* to really digest all the points.

REMEMBER ... "IT ALL STARTS FROM THE START!"

PERFORMANCE TILTS

The way you tilt your spine at address has a huge impact on how you perform your swing.

If you want to create power, you are going to need to start in a strong and balanced position. **You should be able to fight, or hold something heavy, during any part of your golf swing.** This all starts from your posture, which would ideally provide balance and range of motion.

I can't tell you how many times someone has come for a lesson and told me that they weren't flexible. Most people are flexible enough to play reasonable golf. They are just set up in a position that doesn't allow them to use the flexibility that they have.

As humans, we use our spine to rotate – 90 percent of our rotation comes from our thoracic spine. We are very good rotating when we are doing normal everyday things. We never think about how to rotate to pick up something that is on the ground to our side, we just react. When we were younger, wrestling with our siblings or friends, we didn't think – we just reacted. *This* is the trouble with golf. It is not a reactionary start, it is a static start. Because we start statically, we need to set up as if we have to react.

The best way I know how to describe why **most people have difficulty playing golf is because they are trying to perform on a Living Tilt™ vs. a Golfing Tilt™.** Trying to play golf on a Living Tilt minimizes a person's thoracic rotation, better known as shoulder turn. Read on, and I'll explain the difference between a Living Tilt and a Golfing Tilt; and I'll tell you why playing golf from a Living Tilt robs you of rotation and causes back pain.

Living Tilt

Golfing Tilt

LIVING TILT

The Living Tilt is how you stand all day. Your spine is straight up and down in the middle of your body from all views.

Most golfers address a golf ball by standing straight up and simply bending forward until the club touches the ground. This just seems like what you should do with the golf ball on the ground. All you would think you need to do is bend over. The problem is that by doing that you have created a side crunch on your trail side (the right side for the right handed player), because when a person holds a golf club, their trail hand is lower on the club than the target hand. Bottom line, your shoulders are on a tilt while hips are level to the ground; therefore, you have created a side crunch.

This type of posture robs you of thoracic rotation and prevents you from making a proper shoulder/torso turn. The Living Tilt posture is also a cause of lower-back pain, because you are forced to try and rotate with a side crunch in your back.

You cannot effectively side bend and rotate at the same time. Your spine is angry when asked to do such a maneuver – and it lets you know later, when you are popping open the bottle of Advil.

See the Living Tilt Swing Sequence on the next page. I bet you know someone who has a swing that looks like it started on a Living Tilt setup position.

If you make a swing sequence from a Living Tilt posture, your swing may end up looking something like the pictures below.

You can see my body just looks "off" — off balance and uncomfortable. You can tell that the swing motion below will struggle to be repeatable. You can also tell why in the picture prior to impact that I am likely to hit the ball fat, especially with my longer clubs. If you struggle with hitting the ball fat or thin, your posture most likely is a major contributor.

The next part of this book will be based on a concept I call THE GOLFING TILT. It is crucial to your success! Read on …

LIVING TILT SWING SEQUENCE

Pic 1

Pic 2

Pic 3

Pic 4

Pic 5

Pic 6

GOLFING TILT = FORWARD TILT + SIDE TILT

The Golfing Tilt is vitally important; it allows all the things you want to happen in your swing: rotation, balance, weight transfer, maintaining spine angle position, and proper knee flex.

Golf Is known for secrets … everyone has "the secret." I am not going to call this "the secret," because that's tacky and really just a marketing ploy. However, I am here to tell you that the Golfing Tilt is the *answer* to all the pieces of the puzzle that you couldn't put together before in your golf swing.

The Golfing Tilt is paramount to everything else in this book. To achieve the golfing tilt, you have to achieve a tilt in two planes at once. *You must have a forward tilt and a side tilt at the same time.*

The first part of the Golfing Tilt is the Forward Tilt

I am going to give you two drills to get into the proper Forward Tilt before we address the Side Tilt.

FORWARD TILT – DRILL 1

1) Put a shaft down your back between your shoulder blades, touching your head and your tailbone.

2) Keep the shaft in contact with all three contact points as you bend forward from your hip joints. To take your address position, bend forward from your hip joints until you feel your shoulder sockets are over your toes.

(Some people are unable to have their head easily touch the stick when they have the club on their back. If you have some forward head movement, don't tilt your head backward in order to touch the stick. Just maintain contact with the stick with your tailbone and the spine between the shoulder blades so that you don't alter the natural curve in your spine.)

Step 1

Step 2

1) Place the butt of your club in your hip joint, with the club parallel to the ground.
2) Bend forward until the club is on a 45-degree angle. This should put you in a position where your shoulders are over your toes.
3) Extend your arms until the clubhead reaches the ground.

When taking your posture, it is imperative that you get into a good forward tilt first. Ninety percent of the rotation for a human being comes from the thoracic spine. Imagine your vertebrae; they work well when they are sitting on top of one another, in a straight line. In this position, they can effectively rotate.

If you set up by bending from your waist, your spine will be rounded and you won't be able to effectively rotate. If you do try and rotate out of a rounded or side bent spine, some other part of your body has to give so that you can get some movement. This movement angers the spine.

Checkpoints for the Forward Tilt, the first half of the Golfing Tilt:
- Your shoulders should be over your toes.
- You upper arms should hang straight down from your shoulder sockets.
- You should be able to draw a line from your hips to your ankles. If your pockets are too far behind your ankle bones, you have too much weight in your heels to start, and this will influence the start of your backswing.
- The shaft should bisect your belt.

At address you want your shoulders, hips, knees, and feet parallel to your target line. Remember: If you **take care of the straight lines, the curves take care of themselves** ... keep reading, and this will make more sense.

THE SIDE TILT IS THE SECOND HALF OF THE GOLFING TILT

To get into the proper side tilt, you are going to have to tilt your hips at address. The reason we need you to tilt your hips at address is so that your hips are on the same angle as your shoulders at your setup position. Your spine is going to stay in its natural state, but on a tilt. Stick with me – this is for power, fluidity, and less pain.

See the pictures on right. The first picture shows my spine straight up and down, and how I stand most of the day in a Living Tilt. The second picture shows my spine "in a straight line/neutral state," but on a tilt or slant. You spine is happier playing golf out of the position shown in the second picture.

To complete the Golf Tilt, you must move your hips so that they are on the same tilt as your shoulders at address. Once you have gotten into your Forward Tilt, you simply need to lower your back hip/back pocket. When you do this, you may feel a little more flex in the back leg, but it is minimal. This is a very tiny move that makes a *huge* difference. Don't make it a big deal, and make sure to use it to your benefit.

It is my belief that if you are set on a *Golfing Tilt*™ you will be able to use your instincts more effectively. Because golf is not a reactionary start, we have to set up where we could move quickly and in balance if we wanted to. Think of other sports and how the body is positioned; there is evidence of spinal integrity. Throughout this book there will be pictures of other sporting motions showing spinal integrity and spinal tilt.

All human motion is the same; again, you are just a spine and six sets of joints. If we are having a cup of coffee together, we must bend our elbows if we are going to get the cup to our mouth. If we didn't, we would spill coffee all over the place. In regard to human motion, there is a way where the body easily flows and a difficult way where the body gets blocked or hurt. The Golfing Tilt will allow you to add more fluidity to your swing.

It is hard to emphasize how important the Golfing Tilt is for creating a fluid balanced swing that hits good shots.

Take a moment and look at the pictures in the left column and notice how the tilt in my torso and entire spine makes it easy for me to rotate.

It is clear from the pictures that a Side Tilt is crucial for mobility. If you want a better shoulder turn, establish a proper Side Tilt at address. We have all heard that we should "turn around our spine." If you set up with your spine on a tilt away from the target when you turn around your spine, you will be able to get a full shoulder turn without sway.

A picture is worth a thousand words. I am not sure how many frames you could actually take in a single swing, but I know it would be a lot. I think people are visual learners, so really study the ten pictures on the next page – then thank me! I just saved you reading ten thousand words.

Seriously, the pictures on the next page are vitally important for you to have a golf swing that **Flows, with Force and Fly!**

Check points for a good Golfing Tilt:

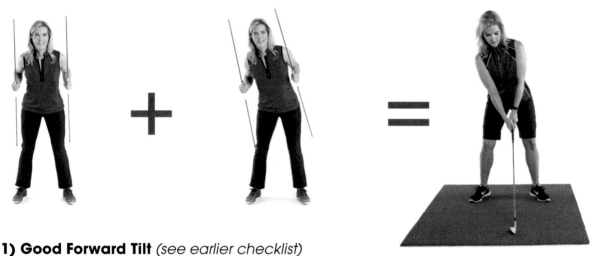

1) Good Forward Tilt *(see earlier checklist)*
2) Proper Side Tilt

- Your back pocket will be lower than your front pocket.
- If you look at yourself in the mirror, your head will be behind your sternum, and your sternum should be behind your zipper.
- Your nose will be directly above your back hip joint, and you will feel like you are looking at the ball from an angle versus directly above.
- Both knees will be flexed and pointing over your toes, which are flared.

The easiest way to think about the Side Tilt is you want your hips and shoulders on the same angle.

Note of caution when practicing: Oftentimes I see students open their hips in relation to the target line at address in an effort to lower their back hip.

It is possible to just lower the back hip while keeping your hips parallel to the target line. You may feel a little more flex in your back leg to achieve a hip tilt while keeping the hips parallel to the target line.

In an ideal setup position, you want your shoulders, hips, knees, and feet parallel to your target line. Remember: If you **take care of the straight lines, the curves take care of themselves.** Keep reading, and this will make more sense.

GOLFING TILT SWING SEQUENCE

The swing sequence below was initiated out of a Golfing Tilt. Notice how mobile and balanced my body and club looks. Throughout the rest of the book, I am going to show you drills and movements so you can develop feels that create a swing that Flows with Force.

Position 1

Position 2

Position 3

Position 4

Position 5

Position 6

BODY PART POSITIONING

Each body part has a function during the swing, and it is important where each part is positioned in the Power Platform™.

On the next page is a checklist for positioning of all six joints, and the major body parts with pictures. The platform is going to be built from the ground up, just as you would lay a solid foundation for building a house. Make sure to put your hands on the club first and then start building your Power Platform from the ground up.

Remember, **Structure Governs Function,** so make sure your body parts are positioned so that you can maximize your range of motion, and maintain balance throughout the swing. Your setup at address dictates how you can move!

If you want to hit it repeatedly and powerfully, master your Power Platform.

EYES Your eyes should be on same tilt at address as your shoulder and hips so that your nose is directly in line with your sternum.

HEAD Your head is an extension of your spine and will be on the same tilt as your spine.

HANDS/GRIP The back of the target hand is the parallel to the target line. The complementary hand is also parallel to the target line. Both hands work in unison with complementary action. The grip will be explained in the next chapter.

ARMS Your upper arms hang straight down out of the shoulder sockets to the elbows. Your forearms will be on a slight slant so that you can grip the club.

ELBOWS Your elbows are slightly bent and pointing off the outer edge of your pockets; you should be able to see your whole chest at address. You never want your elbows locked or for the points of your elbows to be pointing back at your torso.

SPINE The spine remains in its natural/neutral state, and is on two tilts at the start of the swing. Remember, the Golf Tilt equals the Forward Tilt and the Side Tilt.

HIP JOINTS Bend forward from your hip joints until your shoulders are over your toes. The hip joints are vitally important and are what allow you to get into a proper forward tilt without rounding your spine. The back hip joint will be lower than the front hip joint at address and during the backswing.

SHIN & ANKLE BONES Your bones only articulate in straight lines, so you want your shin bones and knee bones to sit vertically on top of the ankle in a straight line. Just like support beams for a house, your legs support your torso. Getting these bones in a straight line determines the width of your stance.

KNEES The knees should have a small amount of flex, and the kneecaps should be pointing in the same direction as the shoelaces/toes. You will feel you have a little more flex in the back knee than the front knee at address, due to the side tilt which requires the back hip to be lower than the front hip.

ANKLES Ankles are positioned directly under the shinbones. You should not feel any pressure in your ankles at address.

FEET The feet should be flared to allow maximum joint movement in the ankles and hips. Weight distribution should be even across the feet, front to back, in the middle of the arches.

STRIKING HANDS: FOR A POWERFUL GRIP

I can't emphasize the importance of the grip enough. How your hands are positioned on the club is vital! You are used to working with your hands in everyday life and don't give those movements a second thought. Therefore, if your hands are gripping the club properly, it is easier for you to use your instincts to square the clubface at impact.

The hands must work in unison! In golf, the hand closest to the target, is the target hand. Many in the golf world call the hand farthest away from the target the trail hand, which is understandable; however, I prefer to call it the Complementary Hand™. When one hand does one movement, the other hand does the complementing action.

Also, your hands must remain in contact with the club at all times. There should be no separation of your hands from the club during the swing. If your hands do come off the club, that's a sign your body is out of position at some point during the swing.

From experience, I know it is easier to get the precise positioning of the grip if you put your hands on the club when it is in the air, versus having the club resting on the ground. I suggest you make a habit of gripping the club in the air before hitting a shot.

Put Up Your Dukes and Come Out Swinging

The title of this book is *Fighting Golf*. I want you to think about how important your hands are when you fight – they are *crucial*! Boxers are taught to make a fist in a certain way so they don't break bones in their hand when they are hitting something. Well, the same holds true for golf.

All golfers may not realize it, but they build their swings around their grip because they have an underlying desire to square the clubface at impact. In order to do that, a golfer with a very strong grip will have to make a swing with different body movements than a golfer with a weak grip.

Your hands affect how the clubface gets squared up at impact. The hands also affect the bones in your wrists and forearms. The more you think about your hands, the more you realize there is only one way to position your hands on the club that is the most powerful and causes less strain.

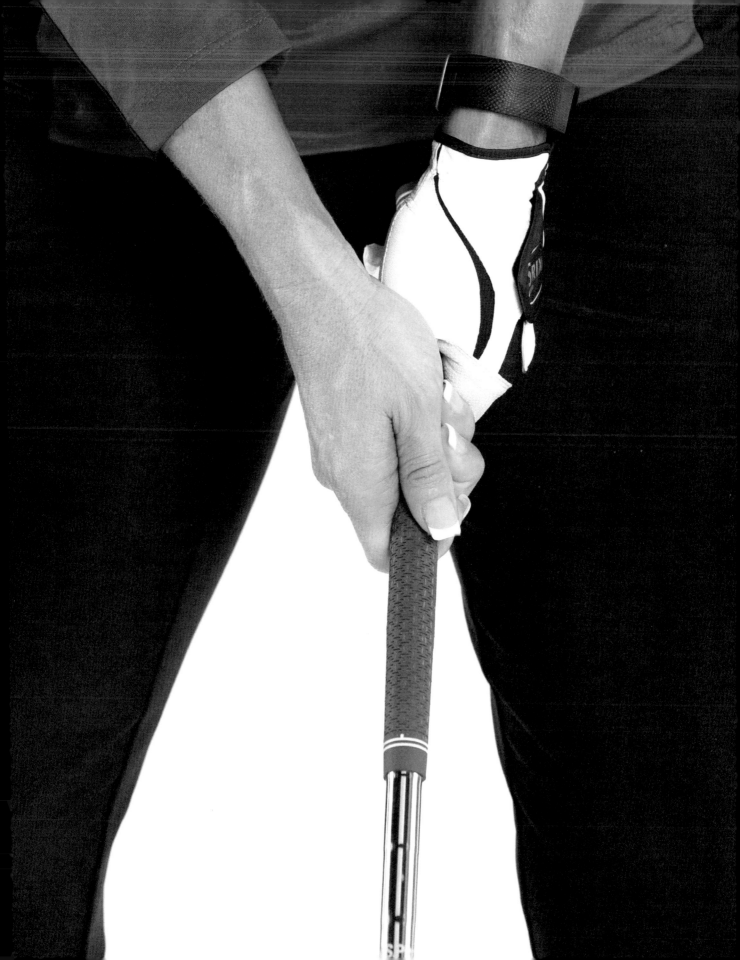

The hand and wrist bones can easily get jammed and hurt during the golf swing, if they are in the wrong position. I want to teach you how to put your hands on the club like you were going to wield a sword or an axe. When you go to grab a weapon, you instinctively put your hands on it in a manner in which you can efficiently hinge your wrists and wield your weapon toward the intended target.

Wherever you are right now reading this book, take a moment and put up your dukes ... go ahead and make a fist. Notice that the back of your left hand is flat. If you were going to hit someone, or backhand something, you would do it with a flat wrist. You wouldn't do it with your hands in a hinged or bowed manner.

Your left hand fist is basically the position of your left hand on the club, if you just lowered your elbow. Take a moment and study the pictures below – notice how getting ready to do some shadow boxing puts you in position to grip a golf club.

If you had to guess a body part that contributes the most speed to the swing, what would you guess that it is? When I ask this question in my lessons the most common answer is the hips. However, according to The Rabito Way, 76 percent of the speed comes from the hinging and unhinging of the wrists. That stat alones stresses the importance of the position of your hands, which determines how effectively the wrists can hinge. The releasing of the wrist hinge is what transfers the energy into the ball. (Carl Rabito and Mike Williams. *Golf: The Rabito Way.* Orlando: CRM of Orlando, 2013. Electronic book.)

For the rest of your life, remember that the **back of the Target Hand is the clubface and the palm of the Complementary Hand is the clubface!**

Your hands and wrists are your force generators, and your grip is the only contact you have with the golf club. If I were you, I would take the time to get most powerful, mobile, air-tight, attacking grip I could.

Now that you understand the importance of the grip, let's learn how to grip it.

TARGET HAND

The Target Hand is the hand that is closest to the target, and has the most contact with the club. There are several positions you are going to want to know to position the club properly in the Target Hand.

Picture 1 – Notice how the club rests in the **"first square,"** the area of the index finger closest to the palm until the knuckle, and on the "**pinky palm bone"** (that's my technical term for the bone that is on the palm of the hand directly below the pinky bone. It feels like a hard marble.).

Picture 2 – The heel pad should be ON TOP of the handle.

Picture 3 – The **thumb** should be resting on the trail half of the handle. And the logo on the glove should be parallel to the target line.

Picture 4 – Is another view of picture 3 and also shows having the heel pad on top of the grip..

 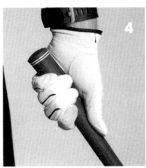

TARGET HAND POSITIONING

1) Put up your dukes and pretend to shadow box. Do this while holding a club in your Complementary Hand, making sure the golf club is on a small slant.

2) Keeping your left fist intact, barely lower your upper arm so it is even with your chest. Now barely open your fingers giving just enough space to slide the club into your Target Hand at an angle. Slide the handle of the golf club into your fist, making sure the golf club is resting from the "first square" to the "pinky bone marble." Close the fist fingers around the club.

See image for where the "First Square" and the "Pinky Palm Bone" are located.

3) Move *only* the thumb, not the palm, so that the thumb is resting down the right half of the shaft. The movement of only the thumb will allow the back of the left hand to remain parallel to the target line.

The club should always look natural in your hands. Notice how my hand looks very comfortable on the club. Humans are built to grip a golf club; all the nooks and creaves in your hand mold beautifully to fit to the club.

Also notice where the back of my forearm is pointing and how my front elbow has comfortable flex in it. It is not straight.

If you can get your hands and arms on without tension, it will allow you to start your swing more fluidly.

Remember, tension kills speed ... and speed is what kills the ball!

When the Target Hand is positioned properly, the back of the left palm or the logo on your glove should be parallel to the target line; you won't be able to see any knuckles on your Target Hand as you look down.

Some in the golfing world may say this is a weak grip, but I am here to tell you it is the *most powerful grip* you can have. Think about how you would backhand something… *always* think about how you would hit something! Your golf club is your tool. It needs to be positioned in your hands so that you can use them to your advantage. **You want to deliver the force, not take the pain!**

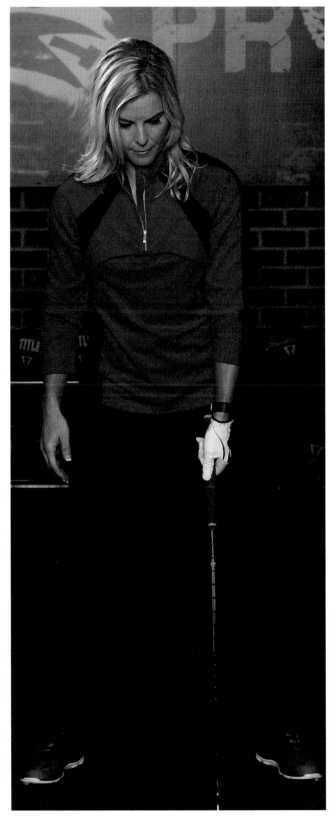

COMPLEMENTARY HAND

The **hand farthest away from the target** is sometimes referred to as the trail hand or the back hand, and it plays a huge part in the swing. You can refer to it however you like; in my mind, I like to think of it as the **Complementary Hand™, because it is the mirror image of the Target Hand**. If the Complementary Hand is in its proper position, it allows the *entire* back arm to work properly, making your swing look good...and resulting in lots of compliments.

For most golfers, the Complementary Hand is their dominant hand; for example, for right-handed golfers, their right hand is their Complementary Hand. (The only time this is different is when a "lefty" plays the game with right-handed golf clubs.)

Positioning and movement of the Complimentary Hand is so important that I almost called it the Control Hand, since for most golfers it is their dominant hand. You typicallly throw a punch or a ball with your dominant hand, and, naturally it plays a huge part in the golf swing. Oddly enough, golf is the one sport that we spend most of our time thinking about our non-dominant hand because it is the one closest to the target, has the most contact with the golf club, and has the glove on it.

From experience, I can tell you the more you understand and master your Complementary Hand, the more the Target Hand is forced to behave. I am sure this is why Ben Hogan once said he wished he had *two* right hands in his golf swing.

Your Complementary Hand is also the hand that most often comes off the club when there is a swing flaw. At all times during the swing, you want constant contact between your hands and the handle of the club. If the Complementary Hand comes off the club, there is a loss of control.

IF YOU WANT A REPEATABLE SWING, YOU MUST START WITH A REPEATABLE GRIP!

In order to position the club properly in the Complementary Hand, you need to be aware of the contact areas on that hand.

CONTACT AREAS OF THE COMPLIMENTARY HAND

DOCKING STATION
The crevasse of the right hand molds into the indentation of the thumb on the front hand.

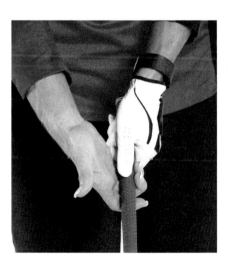

MIDDLE SQUARES
The grip rests in the middle squares of the Complementary Hand.

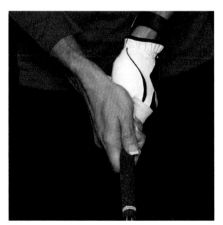

THUMB
Thumb on Complementary Hands rests on the target half of the golf club.

Pinch the thumb and forefinger of the Complementary Hand together. Pinching of those fingers together makes a trap where the shaft can't escape.

WHOEVER NAMED THE GRIPS IN GOLF HAD A SICK SENSE OF HUMOR!

If a golfer has a "traditionally" strong grip, he or she is in a weak position to fight.

Look at the pictures below.

Now let's get you in a position to hit something in a manner that won't hurt your hands and wrists! **Let the punishment of the ball begin!**

HAVE CLUBS THAT FIT YOU?

Earlier in the book, I mentioned that you needed to understand two things before working on the motion of your swing. You need to first understand the collision; second, you need clubs that fit you. Now that you understand the Power Platform and the grip, you should check that your clubs work with your posture.

Most golfers have heard they should have their clubs fitted for them, and this is good advice. As a result, golfers will get fit for clubs because they care about their game; the only problem is most golfers aren't sure what the most important thing is that they should be looking for in the fitting process and how the variables in the club affect their swing.

When you first start the game, the two most important things in your golf club are lie angle and length. If you are looking to use your instincts to compress the ball, it is important for you to have the proper lie angle based off your posture/Power Platform. (The proper posture is covered later in this book.)

The **lie angle** is the angle of shaft relative to the sole of the golf club. Lie angle is important because it affects the direction of the ball, and it affects whether you will have to alter your spine angle or swing path during the swing. If the lie angle doesn't sit properly at address, it forces you to compensate and most likely change your spine angle so that you can make the sole return flat to the ground to give yourself the best chance to hit the ball.

See the pictures below of the different lie angles and their effects.

Heel is off the ground **Influences a shot to the right**	**Club Properly Soled** **Promotes a straight shot**	**Toe in the air** **Influences a shot to the left**
With this kind of lie angle, a golfer must make a compensation in their swing motion to make the ball go straight.	In this game, we all need a little help. Start with good lie angle to make your shot making easier.	With this kind of lie angle, a golfer must make a compensation in their swing motion to make the ball go straight.

The next statement goes against the grain of most golf thought out there. I believe **you must determine the proper lie angle and length of the club** *statically,* **based on a golfer's posture at address.** Most club fits are done dynamically. A dynamic fit is one done with a golfer hitting golf balls. This type of fit may improve your ball striking but you must continue to use the same swing pattern you used during the dynamic fitting to get a decent result. If you try and improve your swing or change your swing motion pattern and your lie angle isn't correct, you are going to run into big trouble.

You might as well learn how to hit the golf ball using a golf club with a proper lie angle based off your good posture. A better lie angle will teach you to get into a better impact position to get a good result. This is especially important for someone new to the game.

Now, on to the fun – how to punish the ball!

So far we have covered the importance of the positioning of your bones, what causes pain during a golf swing, how you place your hands on the club, how you assume the Power Platform, and what to focus on during a club fitting.

The rest of the book will be dedicated to *movement!* And movement is the fun stuff. The focus will be on the Six Striking Positions for a fluid swing that **Flows with Force and Fly!**

POSITION 1

THE GENERATOR

POSITION 1 THE GENERATOR

Because the golf swing is simply a sequence of chain reactions, how you start your swing is crucial! That's why I refer to the start of the swing as The Generator.

Generating lots of speed and power comes from moving your torso properly throughout the swing. After all, your torso is the engine that makes your arms fly. Think about it: if you want to throw a ball farther, you move your chest quicker. If you want to throw a punch harder, you move your chest more forcefully.

The focus of the posture chapter was to get you into a position so you can rev your "torso engine" and generate a smooth swing that purrs with power. So to generate your optimal torso movement, you need to be on a Golfing Tilt.

Ultimately, Position 1 is the checkpoint for the first half of the backswing. At Position 1, a golfer is attempting to:

- Rotate their shoulders 45 degrees so the front shoulder is over the pants zipper.
- Get the club parallel to the ground and the target line at the same time.
- Keep the back hip lower than the front hip.

To get into Position 1, you have to do what I refer to as a Tandem Movement – doing two things at the same time. In this case, you'll need to extend and roll your arms while turning your torso. I'll explain these two parts separately then teach you how to blend them.

TANDEM MOVEMENTS OF POSITION 1

ARM MOVEMENT
In order to balance your club, your arms need to "move and roll."

Allow your back arm to extend away from your body while your upper arm moves off your torso. As your arm moves away from your body, allow your forearms and hands to roll to the point where the clubface is on a "slant" when the club shaft is parallel to the ground in the backswing. Ideally, you want the clubface to be on the same slant as the club shaft started at address. The easiest way to think about this is if you are swinging indoors; the toe of the golf club will be tilted toward the wall behind you when you reach Position 1.

You're probably thinking, "That sounds fairly simple ... just move my arms and hands away. I can do that! So why have I been having so much trouble with my swing?" Most likely, you were moving your hands and arms while forgetting to turn your torso.

Read the next section on the torso movement. If you add good torso movement to your arm/hand movement, good stuff happens!

TORSO MOVEMENT

In order to balance your body properly in Position 1, your torso has to turn properly.

Ideally, a golfer wants to start their swing with a good shoulder turn without sway. This is a daunting task for many golfers. Below describes the sequence of events to generate a back swing start *without* sway.

(For those of you who are new to golf: a SWAY is when your center of gravity moves toward your back leg in the backswing.)

Position 1 calls for a good Torso Turn/Roll. The easiest way to generate a Torso Turn is by pulling back with your back shoulder. Remember, your torso is your engine, and the easiest way to know what your torso is doing is by focusing on your sternum and shoulders. If you start your swing by pulling back with your back shoulder, you'll feel your sternum move closer to your back leg. As you make this motion, you'll start to feel the weight transfer into your back leg as your sternum moves. The movement of the sternum is what is allowing you to feel the weight transfer, and it feels incredibly powerful. You feel like you are loading up to hit something ... which you are!

The proper torso turn affects everything in your golf swing, and it gives the added bonus of maintaining proper flex in both legs during the swing.

What you don't want to do is start the swing by pushing your front shoulder down. This causes your front shoulder to dip, your torso gets off tilt and your back leg straightens. Instinctively, you will start to feel out of balance and weaker in this position versus when you make a proper turn. I refer to this movement as a Torso Rock, which leads to the dreaded "Rock and Block" shot.

So, stop torso rocking and start torso rolling and watch how your swing path improves!

KNOW HOW

DRILLS

The purpose of the drills for Position 1 are to help you elicit a feel and develop body awareness, so you know how to get into a particular position.

All human motion is the same. Each person is comprised of a spine and six sets of joints: shoulders, elbows, wrists, hips, knees, and ankles. How you use your spine and joints dictates how your body moves. And your "feels" are dictated by how your body is moving.

Keep in mind that each joint in your body only has a given range of motion, and if that joint is maxed out, something else has to give. A different body part has to compensate, or a muscle gets stretched so you can do what you are attempting to do. Nothing in your golf swing should hurt or take you beyond your normal range of motion.

Everyone is capable of the movements necessary to make a good golf swing. You know how to make these moves when doing other activities. However, most golfers just haven't put the sequence of these movements in the correct order. I am hoping that by giving you drills you do in your everyday life and showing you how they relate to the golf swing will help you with your game. There may be a few "golfy" drills in this book, but for the most part they will be movements you are familiar with.

DRILLS FOR POSITION 1

There are four drills provided to help you with your chest turn to achieve Position 1. Some motions are hard to put into words. The movement of the hands hinging and rolling is one of those movements that's better to *watch* vs. read about. Go to FightingGolf.com to see how the hands work at the start of the swing.

Different drills resonate with different people, so do the ones you like; this approach will keep your practice fun and effective.

- Throw a Punch
- Pick Up a Heavy Bucket
- Slide the Shaft on a Table
- Tray of Drinks

THROW A PUNCH

The name of this book is *Fighting Golf*. So I want to start this series of drills, for Position 1, with a fighting move.

We have all pretended to shadow box at some point in time. It's fun. We feel alive and feel powerful; that is the feeling you should have before you hit a golf ball.

Stand up and put up your dukes. I want you to notice how your fists and wrists look. They are flat so that they can deliver a forceful blow and absorb the energy resulting from it.

Now I want you to pull back like you are going to throw a punch. Notice your entire chest moved, your elbows are bent ... yes, bent, and you have loaded your back leg. Your back hip is lower than the front hip. Your head is behind your sternum, which is behind your zipper in relation to the target. You have effectively loaded into your back leg ready to transfer all your energy into the punching bag, which is your target. *Now* this is starting to sound like golf!

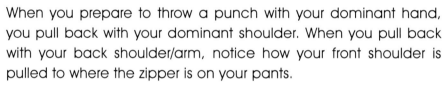

When you prepare to throw a punch with your dominant hand, you pull back with your dominant shoulder. When you pull back with your back shoulder/arm, notice how your front shoulder is pulled to where the zipper is on your pants.

Now take a look at my back when I am halfway back in the backswing. Notice I am tilted *away* from the punching bag/golf target. I am loading up to knock the stuffing out of that ball.

Notice the similarity between throwing a punch and Position 1. You wouldn't think of throwing a punch without turning your chest. If you attempted to throw a punch with just your arm, without a torso turn, it would feel weak and terrible.

Allow your inner warrior to start the swing!

PICK UP A HEAVY BUCKET

In your golf swing, you should be in a position to hold a heavy weight or fight at any position during your swing.

Position a basket of balls on a chair or stool as shown in the picture below. The rim of the bucket is at mid-thigh height.

Now I want you to turn and pick up the bucket and bring it to the front of you.

Do that motion a few times; while you are moving, notice your body positioning. You are pretty darn close to the start of a perfect backswing.

You probably noticed that you didn't have your legs moving all around and you *didn't* stretch your arms to get the bucket. You turned your chest to square up to the bucket, then you used your arms to get the bucket.

If you keep doing this motion repeatedly, you will feel how your core and ribcage are working. If you add a little weight to the bucket, you will start to get a little bit of a core workout and will realize where your torso should be when you are in your strongest position.

Now whenever you are doing your laundry, you can work on your golf swing. I sure do!

UPPER BODY
- The shoulders TURN to face the bucket.
- The left shoulder has moved from its starting position.
- Notice the position of your hands. They are natural; they are not excessively open or closed.

LOWER BODY
- Your legs are stable underneath you.
- The back hip is lower than the front hip.
- Both feet are firmly on the ground
- There has been a weight transfer to the back leg.
- The head is behind the sternum which is behind the zipper in relation to the golf target.

The motion of grabbing a bucket of balls to the side of you or a laundry basket is the same movement that is needed to get into the first position in your golf swing.

TRAY OF DRINKS

Imagine you are having a party with a bunch of friends, and you have gone to get a tray of drinks for the table. This can be any beverage you wish: water, soda, spirits, or anything else that you like to drink.

For this drill, you will need a dinner tray or a balance board as displayed here. The "tray" will need a little bit of weight to it and needs to be positioned on the upper portion of your pecs, pressing against your chest. Pretend that the tray is full of drinks and that you have to start your turn without letting the drinks fall off the tray.

If you turn back correctly, you will be able to effectively start the turn in your backswing and then be able to pass the drinks. If you turn incorrectly at the start of the backswing, all the drinks crash to the floor … major party *and* golf flaw that needs to be avoided.

In each drill I give you, I want you to notice the similarities in the body positioning of what you do in everyday life, in other sports, and in your golf swing.

A good shoulder turn allows my legs to stay stable – a poor shoulder turn forces me to drop the drinks and my front leg to crumble.

From this starting position, you can either drop the drinks on the floor or get the drinks to the table and let the fun begin! At the start of the swing, you have options.

Good Position:
If the front shoulder is level to the ground, everyone gets to have a drink.

Poor Position:
If the front shoulder dips, all the drinks fall to the floor ... lots of thirsty people.

TABLE SLIDE

I love this drill because it really gets you in tune with the torso movement in the golf swing.

Grip your golf club and hinge *just your wrists* until the shaft of the club is parallel to the ground. Now pretend that you are going to slide the club across a coffee table until the shaft is in line with your hands from the down-the-line view. It's that simple to get into Position 1 if your torso turns properly.

When doing this drill, let your torso be the engine for everything. Once you have hinged your wrists, all you have to do is turn your chest to get into Position 1. Do not stretch your hands away or let your arms cross your chest. Notice that my upper arms are still hanging straight down out of my shoulder sockets. If everything moves in sequence, your arms will remain at your sides as you turn.

As you get more comfortable with doing this drill, once you have gotten into Position 1, you can finish the rest of the swing. You might be surprised how well you hit it when doing this drill.

CHECKPOINTS — POSITION 1

There are no shortcuts to Position 1. If you shortchange your chest turn at the start of the swing, it will force some other part of your body to try and make up the slack.

BODY CHECK
Upper Body
- The chest moves 45 degrees so that the front shoulder is in line with the zipper.
- The torso turns as upper arms are still on the sides of your torso.
- The arms do not stretch across the chest.
- The elbows each have some flex.
- The head has stayed in place and is on the same tilt as address.

Lower Body
- The back hip is lower than the front hip.
- Your feet should be grounded and the knees should be wide.
- Your front knee will have moved a bit toward your back leg, and has the same amount of flex as it did at address.

CLUB CHECK
Clubface
The clubface has the toe slightly behind the heel – the clubface will be on a similar "slant" as the shaft plane at the start.

Club Shaft
The golf club is parallel to the ground on the backswing and parallel to the target line.

"THERE ARE NO SHORT CUTS TO ANYPLACE WORTH GOING."
—BEVERLY SILLS

It is my belief that the number one reason most amateurs struggle with their swing is that they aren't moving their torso properly during the swing; as a result, they are out of balance and in a weak position.

Once a golfer has initiated a side crunch in their torso at the start of the swing, they are forced into a series of movements in order to create some sort of playable shot. They know in their subconscious something was "off," but they aren't sure how to fix it. This swing uncertainty is why so many golfers struggle with confidence and worry about losing their swings.

Initiating the wrong torso movement at the start of the swing also adds more stress to the body.

Keep reading - you are about to find more answers to a more balanced, powerful repeatable swing.

P.S. Be patient with yourself as you work on any swing change. You have to give your mind a chance to develop body awareness and timing of the new move.

▶ ▶ ▶ ▶ ▶ **STUDENT INSIGHT:** David Ashton, USMC – "Position 1 is the most important. If I can get there smoothly, the rest of the swing creates itself. The only positions I practice getting into are Position 1 and Position 2. I let my body take care of the rest; mentally it is like dominos falling for me."

When David started working with me he was shooting in the mid 80s. We had 14 lessons over 18 months and he shot 72 ... and now regularly shoots in the 70s. He has also started to win local tournaments!

You are about to start reading about Position 2, which is the top of the backswing. There are a large number of golfers who are obsessed with the top of their backswings. I can't tell you how many times I have heard, "If I could just get into the slot at the top, I know I would hit a good shot." There is a lot of merit to this concern, so let's go figure out the top of your backswing.

POSITION 2

READY TO WIELD

POSITION 2 READY TO WIELD

This chapter teaches you how to get to the **top of your backswing** so you will be **Ready to Wield** your golf club, in balance with speed, at that defenseless little ball.

Let me ask you a question: How do you think the club gets to the top of your backswing?

If you said you have to *lift* your arms, you are a candidate for over swinging, reverse pivoting, straightening the back leg, and a whole host of other things. If you said *bend* your elbows ... ding ding ding! You are correct. Yes, I did say *bend*. (Your elbows are your best friends – go to FightingGolf.com for more information.) Your elbows are force levers; *use them*!

Flip back to POSITION 1 for a minute and notice that the shoulders have turned 45 degrees and the club shaft is parallel to the ground. In order to get to the top of the swing, Position 2, you should allow your elbows to bend. This will allow for you to complete your shoulder turn to a full 90 degrees.

Whenever you lock out your elbows during the swing, it stops the rotation of the spine. Since the spine has been blocked by the locked elbows, another body part or muscle has to compensate to get you to the top of your swing. This type of move usually adds more stress to the body as you swing.

Purpose of the Position 2
The purpose of Position 2/the top of the backswing is to put you into position to deliver a blow to the golf ball. You are truly getting ready to wield the weight. You want to be in a place where your hands can travel back on the same path they went up, which is the most efficient way to return the clubface. Think about it: If you were chopping something that was on the ground, you would use the same hand path on the way up and the way down.

In the chapter discussing Position 1, we discussed the tandem movements of the shoulder and arm movements at the start of the swing. **In Position 2, the major movement pieces are the elbows bending and the completion of the shoulder/torso turn.**

The bending of the **elbows** allows you to complete your backswing and allows the back hip joint to stay lower than the front hip.

The **torso** turn from Position 1 to Position 2 should be simple. It is paramount you focus on keeping your torso on the proper tilt and height from the ground. After all, what is attached to your torso – your head, ding, ding, ding! If you don't want to have your head lift, your torso can't raise in the backswing. In the following pages you will see how the torso should be positioned at the top of the swing.

Where should the wrists be at the top of the swing?

There is always considerable discussion as to where the target arm wrist should be at the top of the backswing. At the end of the day, when we play golf, we are just chopping with a stick— chopping and turning, chopping and turning.

Anytime you put something in your hands in order to make a chopping motion, your wrists go from flat to cupped.

There has also been much discussion in golf about when and where the wrists should be cupped and when they should be flat. In my mind, it is as simple as chopping wood.

Take a moment and look at the pictures of me making a chopping motion below.
At the top of any chopping motion there will be a "cup" in each wrist. In my mind, the cups connote strength and will help you apply more force into the ball while reducing the strain on the wrists at the top of the backswing. In a chopping motion your wrists start flat; they cup to create energy, and they go back to flat when the energy is released. The same thing should happen in your golf swing.

Side Note
One of my students doesn't like the words "cup" or "hinge" and refers to this movement as having a "dent" in each wrist … so go make some dents!

At the top of your backswing, you should feel balanced and strong. You should also be able to hold this position for a long period of time.

You should also be able to fight off two opponents, one on each side of you, at the same time. You should be able to punch an attacker at the top of your backswing and kick an attacker coming toward you from the target line. (If you are truly kicking something, lead with your heel. For the golf ninja you just have to get your leg in the air.) If you are balanced, you can do it! I call this move the **Golf Ninja™**.

You can actually hit a golf ball doing the Golf Ninja move, but you will have to go to **FightingGolf.com to see the Golf Ninja in action**. The Golf Ninja move is just as fun as doing the Happy Gilmore but doesn't require a running start.

KNOW HOW

There are five drills listed below for Position 2.

Throw a Golf Upper Cut
Hold Off an Intruder
Rest, Turn, and Set
Chop, Chop – Side Chop
Target Arm Hang Check

FIGHT AND THROW!
Golf is just a combination of fighting, chopping, and throwing.

Look at the pictures on this page, and you can see the strength in these people. You can easily imagine how they got into those positions. Notice that none of the people look contorted. And also notice that they are all tilted away from their intended target so they can propel an object toward their target.

In regard to the warrior with the sword, I'm just scared of him ... and the ball will be scared of you if you get into a balanced and loaded Position 2.

THROW A GOLF UPPER CUT

Get in a stance with your dukes up and start shadow boxing by throwing uppercuts. When you are shadow boxing and throwing uppercuts, your hand will finish in front of your face. Amend that motion just a little to make it applicable to golf. When you throw a Golf Upper Cut, your hand/punch will finish just outside the opposite shoulder.

Look at the pictures below. To make this boxing uppercut motion applicable to golf, imagine you are throwing an upper cut to a bag located just outside your back foot and just behind your back heel. When you hit the bag, your target hand will be even with your ear – this is where you would like to be at the top of your backswing.

Again, notice how your body works in unison to achieve your goal of hitting the punching bag. Your chest turns, your elbows bend, and your legs are stable while weight was transferred to your back leg. Again, you feel balanced, powerful, and comfortable … a recipe for a good golf swing.

With your lead hand, you will feel like you are throwing the punch under and up.

HOLD OFF AN INTRUDER

Good golfers have good imaginations. They use their imaginations to create images, analogies, and metaphors that get themselves into certain body positions. These body positions allow them to create the "feels" they use when they play. For this drill, if you are by yourself, you will have to use your imagination. If you have a friend around, then try this drill for real.

As stated before, ideally when you are fighting you are balanced, and you have your body in a position of leverage. I want you to feel that you are balanced and loaded at the top of your backswing so that you can deliver a smooth forceful blow to the ball.

To start this drill, get into your Power Platform posture position. Now you have to imagine that you have to fight off an intruder to the side of you on your back leg. For the purposes of this drill, leave your toes facing the ball so you only have the ability to turn your torso to fend off an intruder. (Basically, pretend you are encased in cement from the thighs down.)

If you make this movement correctly, you will be in the position to fight or knock the intruder down. You will notice that your head is behind your sternum, and your sternum is behind your zipper. You must keep your back hip down so that you have the leverage to push the intruder. Once the back hip starts to rise, you have lost the leverage and given the advantage to the intruder, the bad guy, or the double bogey man, who in this case could knock you over.

See the pictures on the next page demonstrating how to hold off an intruder and how it looks similar to the top of the backswing.

Common Power Leak – One of the biggest flaws I see in golfers is that they are trying to get their arms as high in the sky as possible. When they do this, it forces their upper arms above their shoulder sockets, which forces the back hip to rise in the backswing. Once they lift their arms, they lose the power they were hoping to gain ... silly game!

Not recommended: You will lose the battle.

Recommended: You win! Intruder is whimpering on the ground.

WHEN YOU LEVERAGE YOUR GOD-GIVEN STRENGTH, YOU MAXIMIZE YOUR POWER.

REST, SET, AND TURN

Use this four-step process to get into a good backswing.

Step 1: Get into your Power Platform setup position addressing a golf ball. Always make sure you are on a Golfing Tilt.

Step 2: From there, just bend your elbows so that the shaft of the golf club is resting on your right shoulder.

Step 3: Now, turn your chest 90 degrees into the backswing, leaving the club on your shoulder while your chest turns.

Step 4: Once you have finished your chest turn, raise your hands slightly back on an angle so that your hands are just behind your back shoulder. The club shaft will be pointing slightly away from you at the top of the backswing.

From here you should be in a very good backswing position, and you can swing through to your finish. Do this a number of times so you can sense the checkpoints for how to get into Position 2.

Each time you do the drill, get in tune with the movement of your torso and how your elbows maintain some sort of flex. It would feel weird to stretch your arms straight and over your head from picture 3 to picture 4.

In your swing, you want to stay powerful and connected; this requires having flex in your elbows and knees. In order to do this, it is helpful to hinge both wrists at the top of the swing.

"ONE MUST ALWAYS PRACTICE SLOWLY.
IF YOU LEARN SOMETHING SLOWLY, YOU FORGET IT SLOWLY."
–ITZHAK PERLMAN

STEP 1

STEP 2

STEP 3

STEP 4

CHOP CHOP

The side chop drill is designed for you to see where you naturally position your hands to deliver a blow into an object on the outside of your back foot.

Whenever you are in a forceful position to chop something, there is a small cup, or "dent," in each wrist. If you go to chop something and make one of the wrists "flat," the club will go off on an angle, making it more likely that you miss your intended target. You are also much weaker if the wrists are bowed or curved.

To work on this drill, put a golf ball in front of you and pretend you are going to chop it in half. As you go to make a chopping motion, notice that you start hinging your wrists and bending your elbows simultaneously. No one needed to teach you how to get into a position to chop wood or kill a poisonous snake that wants to bite you.

SIDE CHOP

For the second half of this drill, get into Position 1 and make chopping motions to the top of your swing, then let the clubhead make contact with a point outside your back foot, even with your shoe laces on the ground. See the pictures below.

The beauty of this drill is it keeps you in your spine angle, and it gets you to see how you will hinge and unhinge your wrists with force. The only way for the club to reach the ground is for the back hip to be lower. If the back hip raises, you will be unable to get the club to reach the floor, and if you do it will look contorted … either that, or you are triple-jointed!

TARGET ARM HANG DRILL

For this drill, all you have to do is swing to the top of your backswing, and stop.

Continue holding the club at the top of your backswing in your Complementary Hand/ Back Hand and let your Target Arm dangle like a heavy rope.

If you have turned your chest properly, your Target Arm will be hanging in front of your back leg. If you have not turned properly into the backswing, your Target Arm will be hanging on your front leg.

Not recommended

The chest is the engine of the swing. If you can get the chest turn initiated correctly at the top of the swing, you are much more likely to be able to rotate back toward the ball powerfully with no strain.

If you have turned properly, you will feel more weight in your back leg – you will feel loaded. If you haven't turned properly, your front shoulder will still be over your front leg. *Reminder: To get into a powerful backswing where you can make a good shoulder turn without sway, you must *must* set up in the Golfing Tilt.

Ideal shoulder turn

CHECKPOINTS — POSITION 2

BODY CHECK
Upper Body
- Your shoulders will move another 45 degrees to complete a 90 degree turn.
- The front shoulder should be over the back leg.
- Elbows are bent with the hands even with the head – *not* above the head!
- Hands outside the back shoe and even with the ears. (front on view)
- Upper arm below shoulder socket.
- Backside of the face even with the outside of the back thigh.

Lower Body
- Back hip lower than the front hip.
- Flex in both legs.
- Grounded on both feet.
- Entire spine on a tilt away from the target.
- Weight shifted into the back leg, feeling more weight in the back right heel.

CLUB CHECK
Clubface
The clubhead is above the hands.
The clubface is on plane – the clubface is on a slant.

Club Shaft
The clubhead will be slightly behind your hands from the down-the-line view.
The shaft is on a "slight tilt" away from you and on an easy "track/slot" to get back to the ball.

MASTER BEING A GOLF NINJA, AND WATCH YOUR BALL STRIKING IMPROVE! YOU WILL START KICKING THE GOLF BALL'S BUTT ... AND HAVE FUN WATCHING IT FLY!

TOP OF BACKSWING
BALANCED AND READY TO STRIKE

▶▶▶▶▶▶ TIFFBIT

Golfers fear losing their swings. Every golfer has had that thought at some time or another. It is a normal concern. If you want to feel confident in your swing, you have to change how you practice and master the little details slowly so you can do all the moves together quickly. Some golfers think it doesn't count as a "rep" if you aren't going fast. You can do as many "reps" as you want, once you figure it out.

"IN ALL THINGS – SPORTS, DANCE, FOOTBALL,
WEIGHTLIFTING, OR BOXING – FORM MATTERS."

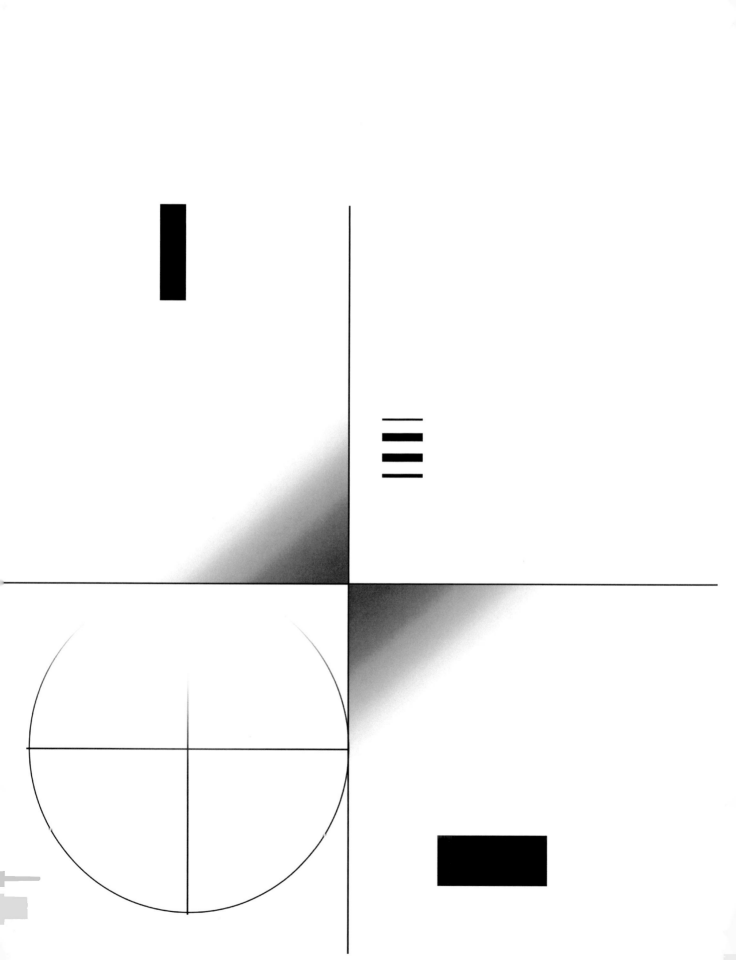

POSITION 3

THE DECISION POINT

POSITION 3 THE DECISION POINT

Position 3 is critical to setting up impact! In my mind, it is so critical I call it the Decision Point.

As mentioned earlier, the clubhead is nothing more than a weight; that weight in motion always wins. Wherever the golf club is when it is parallel to the ground on the downswing dictates what you must do in order to make a strike on the ball; that is why I call it the Decision Point.

Ideally you would like for the golf club to be parallel to the ground and parallel to the target line at the same time, with your upper arms hanging straight down out of the shoulder sockets. When the club is in this position, your club is in balance and primed for a center-face hit. This position also allows for the clubhead to travel down the target line for a few inches after impact, helping create straight solid shots – and those much sought-after bacon strip divots.

Because the downswing is happening so quickly, your choices are dictated for you if your club is out of balance at this point. If your club is out of balance and you kept swinging the club on the path it was on without making a body compensation, you would hit a poor shot – or even whiff. **Remember, if the club gets out of position, you have to make a maneuver with your body to attempt to get the clubhead back in position to save the shot.**

The trick to getting into Position 3 is feeling more activity out of your chest than your legs. I know most of us have been conditioned that the hips create most of the speed in the golf swing and they are a huge contributor for the amount of force you can deliver into the ball. However, most people are using their hips too early in the swing to get the most benefit from them. It is crucial to know *how* and *when* you use your hips.

Later in this chapter I will provide drills to teach you how to coordinate your upper and lower body by focusing more on the torso. Focusing on the torso at the start of the downswing is a fairly novel concept for golf instruction since the majority of golf instruction puts a huge focus on the hips at the start of the downswing.

When I first started learning golf, the discussions of the hip movement would melt my brain. There was talk of figure eights and rubber bands – none of it made any sense to me. (For the record, if you have read a lot of golf books … you are not a rubber band. If you were, you could never stop during any position in your golf swing because you would just "snap" right back. And I have not yet seen golfers flying around the range because they "pulled back" and let go.)

Even though the torso approach is fairly rare, I believe you will find it very beneficial and easier on your body.

The Transition – The Movement out of Position 2 to Position 3
In order to be more in control at Position 3 and be the "decision maker" who controls that little white ball; a golfer has to work on the transition of their golf swing out of Position 2 down to Position 3.

As stated earlier, all golfers need good imaginations. Therefore, I want you to think of yourself as a golf ball assassin during the first part of your downswing. The first part of the downswing should be smooth, like you are sneaking up on the golf ball so that you can kill it. There are no sudden motions from the top of the backswing; ideally the hands come back down the same path they went up … that is if you have mastered Positions 1 and 2, of course.

Remember, golf is a game of leisure, and the transition should be easy. The transition is where the momentum for the speed just slowly gathers. Once the clubhead reaches parallel to the ground, that is where the speed really picks up and where the back leg comes into play.

Each position in the swing is extremely important – otherwise we wouldn't be talking about it – however, Positon 3 is the last segment before striking the ball. Where you are at this point dictates what you must do in order to make contact and not whiff the ball.

The Grip and The Posture Platform are non-negotiable in the making of a Fighting Golfer. After that, Positions 1, 2, and 3 are where you should spend most of your time practicing because they really set up impact. Where you are at Position 3 dictates what must happen for the rest of the swing because **The Weight Always Wins!**

KNOW HOW

DRILLS FOR POSITION 3

Four drills are provided to help you feel what a smooth transition will feel like and get you into Position 3, so you can deliver a blow onto the golf ball.

Point Down the Tunnel
How to Use Your Butt
Buttocks Behavior
Ruled for Precision

The golf swing is very complex set of actions happening in a short time span. On the PGA Tour, the average swing takes one second, with the backswing taking 0.75 seconds and the downswing taking 0.25 seconds. For any golfer, it is very difficult to know exactly what happened in the downswing when you are swinging at full speed.

Due to the fact that the downswing happens so quickly, and body awareness is the only way to truly improve, I am *obsessed* with players learning how to do demonstrations and slow motion drills perfectly. You must be able to do a demonstration or slow motion swing properly at extremely slow speed so that you can learn to swing through these positions quickly for their maximum strike.

"TO CHANGE A HABIT, MAKE A CONSCIOUS DECISION, THEN ACT OUT THE NEW BEHAVIOR."
—MAXWELL MALTZ

POINT DOWN THE TUNNEL...
to wrap up great shots!

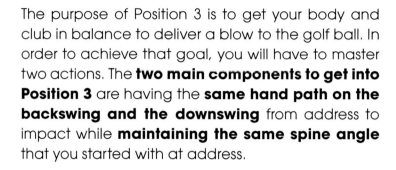

The purpose of Position 3 is to get your body and club in balance to deliver a blow to the golf ball. In order to achieve that goal, you will have to master two actions. The **two main components to get into Position 3** are having the **same hand path on the backswing and the downswing** from address to impact while **maintaining the same spine angle** that you started with at address.

Learning how to point the grip down a tunnel parallel to your target line will help you achieve both of those objectives and master Position 3.

To set up this drill, you will need some items that you can get at any office supply store or may already have in your home. You will need three to four plastic file crates as seen below and a tube of wrapping paper. You will need to position the file crates vertically until one of them is at your hand height. Then place the wrapping paper tube in the slot of the file crate that is even with your hands.

Once you have the items in place, take your setup and make sure that the back of your Target Hand is pointing toward the wrapping paper and the end of the gift wrapping tube in the middle of the front thigh. When you swing back to Position 1, your chest should move but not your legs, so the end of the giftwrapping tube will still be in the middle of your front thigh.

Now swing to the top of your swing and stop. From here your entire focus should be on getting the end/butt of the grip to point through the gift wrapping role, i.e., the "tunnel." At this point, your club will be both parallel ground and the target line at the same time – perfect Position 3.

The only way to get the end of the grip/"light" shining through the tunnel is to follow the proper hand path on the down swing and the clubhead would have to be in line with the hands from the down-the-line view and parallel to the target line.

You will also notice that your legs are still stable and strong under you. The back leg is in the same position at setup, and during Positions 1, 2, and 3. Also, you had to maintain your spine angle.

If making the training aid is too much work and you just want to work on the concept, go get one of cardboard middles from either a paper towel roll or toilet paper roll. You can rest the "roll" on a stool or a table that is approximately the proper hand height and be able to tell how you will need to move your hands and torso to point the butt of the club through the center of the roll.

Golf is an exhilarating and challenging game, so improving at golf should be equally entertaining.

HOW TO USE YOUR BUTT!

There is a lot of talk about your butt in the golf swing. And I am guessing you have heard some of these gems below:

Stick Your Butt Out!

Honestly, I don't want to play *any* sport where I have to stick my butt out – first off, that's weird, and second, it makes it difficult to make a good backswing because it puts you out of balance. When you have a good golf posture, your pants look tight across your buttocks but *not* because you stuck your butt out. By virtue of bending forward from your hip joints, your pants will be taut on your rear, giving the *appearance* you stuck your butt out – but you didn't.

Feel Like Your Butt is Sitting on a Bar Stool

Now that you know how to get into the Posture Platform, you will never think about sitting on a bar stool again – during a golf swing that is – for two reasons. One, there are no bar stools on the golf course, just at the 19th hole. And two, if you are thinking about sitting on bar stool to get into your address position, you will have too much knee flex and too much weight on your heels.

Keep Your Butt on the Wall

This piece of "golf advice" always confused me. When I was first playing, I had a golf friend tell me that I should keep my butt on the wall during the swing. I laughed ... but heck, we will all try anything to hit it better. So I stood next to that stupid wall for hours and couldn't figure out where the club should go. If I started to swing back, all I did was scrape the wall – and then I felt like an idiot, with my butt on the wall with the golf club in a vertical and awkward position at the top of the backswing.

After years of thought, I now know what this friend meant. The wall is a good analogy – you just can't use a normal wall; you have to use a half wall. I am going to help you learn how to use your butt, but we are going to use something other than a wall. We are going to use some mobile crates ... turn to the next page. Good golfers have command of their butts!

BUTTOCKS BEHAVIOR

What function does your butt really play in the golf swing?

Your glutes/butt are the largest and most powerful muscle group in your body. You need to have control over your butt in order to hold your posture and create maximum power when you make your turn in the golf swing. To master your butt positioning during the swing, do this drill.

Use the same mobile crates discussed in the previous drill "Point Down the Tunnel". Stack the crates to the point where they are just under your butt bones when you take a setup position.

When you move into Position 1, your chest will move while both butt bones remain on the crate. As you move into Position 2, your target side butt bone will come off the crate, but your trail side butt bone will still be on the crate.

Now, as you transition into Position 3, your front butt bone will return to the crate but will not touch the same place it started at address. Instead, it should touch the crate about a golf ball width closer to the target. This movement will ensure a proper weight shift. At Position 3, both butt bones will be on the crates and you may feel like your trail buttocks slid across the crate a bit as the front leg/butt moved. At the same time in Position 3, the shaft of the club is positioned parallel to the target line just prior to impact.

Once your front butt bone returns to the crate at Position 3, your trail of side of the body can finish the swing. As you turn to the finish, you will feel some sort of contact with the crate on your front leg. You will feel your front leg turn on the crate from the butt bone to the side of the hip.

Recommended: Proper buttocks action from Set-up to Position 3. Notice that the better buttocks motion allows you to keep flex in both legs. It also promotes a better swing path.

Not Recommended: Below are pictures of a non-desired buttocks movement caused by poor torso movement at the start of your swing. Notice how the back leg gets straight in the photos below. It also promotes and "over the top" move.

If you figure this out, without props, you are a genius! It took me forever to do this. Save tons of time and countless hours of awkward contortions by checking out the movement at www.FightingGolf.com. Still pictures are helpful, but it is best if you can see the entire swing sequence.

RULED FOR PRECISION

I want to stress one huge point. Position 1 & Position 3 are similar in the fact that the club is parallel to the ground for both positions but the *location of the hands is different.* At Position 1, your hands are outside your back leg, and at Position 3 the hands should be in front of the back leg or between the legs.

When you swing, you want to imagine that you are flowing through the "shaft line" you created at Position 1 with the focus of getting the hands in front of your back leg at Position 3. In order to make your most efficient strike, the clubhead needs to be on plane at positon Position 1 & Position 3. Yes, I just said *clubhead,* the **clubhead needs to be on plane**. Generally we only hear about the shaft being on plane, but having the clubface on plane is vital as well!

In order to have the clubface on plane, the clubface at Position 1 & Position 3 must be on the same/similar slant as the club shaft at address. (Refer to the Checkpoints pages at the end of the chapter for Positon 1 and Position 3 and look at the clubface position.)

This drill will primarily be done at home. It cements into your subconscious what you are attempting to do and how you are going to get there. I am a firm believer that the best "golf work" is done at home, not on the course. In school, if you did your homework, you usually figured things out and got smarter. The same thing goes for your golf game: If you spend time at home looking at relationships between your club and your body, you start to figure things out. You will only be able to trust your swing on the golf course if you *completely* understand your swing and how your body works.

Take the mobile crates and stack them until your hands at address are in middle of one of the crates. Take two rulers/yardsticks and position them through the holes in the crates as shown on the next page. Make sure the rulers are on a slant when you set them up.

In order to get your clubface to swing through the rulers your clubface will have to be on a slant; i.e., on a plane. Work on doing this drill, and you'll notice you're forced to make the same hand path on the way back and the way down to get through the rulers.

Errors – If your hands go away from you at the start of the down swing, you will hit the outside ruler.

Error – If the clubface is closed, it can't get through the rulers either on the backswing or the downswing.

BAD
Closed Clubface won't make it
through the rulers.

GOOD
Clubface is on a slant and will fit
through the rulers.

CHECKPOINTS — POSITION 3

BODY CHECK

Upper Body
- Your hands are in front of the back leg or between your legs.
- Elbows are still bent.
- Your spine is tilted slightly away from the target.
- The shoulders start to unwind with the front shoulder approaching the front leg.
- The chest is facing the ground on the same angle as at address; therefore, you maintain your spine angle.

Lower Body
- Legs are flexed and knees wide.
- Your front foot is firmly on the ground and the back foot is starting to push off.

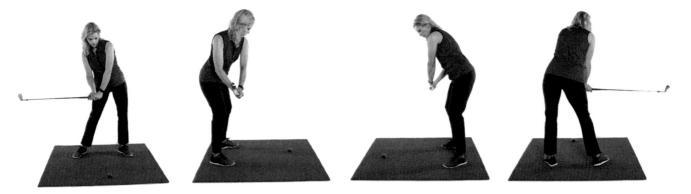

CLUB CHECK
Clubface
- The clubface is on plane, meaning the clubface will be on a small slant with the toe of the golf club being slightly behind the heel.

Club shaft
The club shaft is parallel to the ground and the target line.

"IT IS IN YOUR MOMENTS OF DECISION THAT YOUR DESTINY IS SHAPED."
-TONY ROBBINS

SAME WITH YOUR GOLF SHOTS, THE DECISION YOU MAKE AT POSITION 3 LARGELY INFLUENCES THE DESTINY OF YOUR GOLF SHOT.

You can see I have some mean intentions on my face. I have made a **Decision** to clobber that ball.

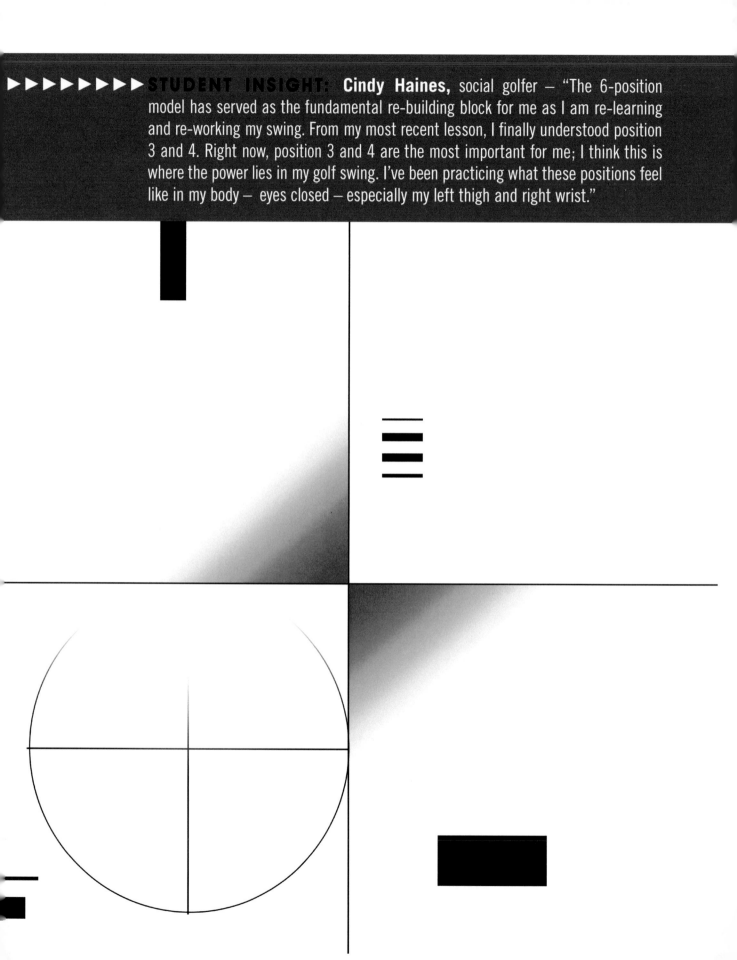

THE COLLISION

KNOWLEDGE

POSITION 4 THE COLLISION

Position 4 is just past impact. The picture on the prior page shows the body and the club at the exact moment of impact. In my world, I call it the *Collision*.

We all want a perfect impact position, but we can't think about it. I have found through experience you will have more success if you think *just past impact* vs. thinking about actual impact. Just like when you throw a punch you want to hit **through** your intended target for full force. You don't want to hit *at* the ball; you need to swing *through* the ball. If you are making a good move in your golf swing, the hit happens anyway. In the golf swing, the golf ball just happens to be at the wrong place at the wrong time. If we think of swinging *through* the ball versus *at* the ball, the results tend to be better.

The image of swinging through the ball also helps you with your weight transfer to the front foot. The easiest way I know how to tell you to get into Position 4 is to view the golf swing like a race. In the race, the finish line is the inside portion of the target leg. The two competitors in the race are your hands and the clubface. In this race, you always want to root for the hands; you always want your hands to win the race, with the hands getting to the left leg before the clubhead. This will ensure a hit in a downward manner.

If the clubhead wins the race, your hands and wrists will be forced into that "flippy" or "scoopy" motion everyone hates. You will also get lots of other undesirable things if the clubhead wins the race, such as thin shots or shots that go to the left because the club-face is forced to close though the impact area.

Transitioning from Position 3 to Position 4 again has two parts, your body and the club. In regards to your body, you ideally you want to "feel" all of your weight on the front leg just past impact. Your head, sternum, and zipper will all be moving closer to your front foot as you move from Position 3 to Position 4. Your goal for the club at Position 4 is to get the clubhead traveling down the target line from the golf ball to just past your front foot.

KNOW HOW: The drills on the following pages will help you learn to **Win the Race!**

DRILLS: Knock Down the Door, Push a Board, Sweep the Floor, Footwork for Force

The Collision

The Finish Line

KNOCK DOWN THE DOOR

Most golfers have heard about posting onto their front leg. I want to show you how to do this properly, and I would prefer for you to view your front leg as your "turn leg" instead of your "post leg."

Terminology is important in golf as it gives your body images for how to perform. I personally don't like the idea of a "post" because a post doesn't move. Some golfers think that in order to post on their front leg they need to excessively straighten or "pop" their front knee/leg, which adds extra stress to the knee. Instead, think of your front leg as your Turn Leg. You will need to transfer almost all of your weight to your front leg so you can effectively turn the rest of your body around that leg so it can face the target.

When a golfer is in a good position just past impact, the majority of their weight will be on their front foot. From a face-on view, the front/turn leg will appear to be in a straight line. However, if you look at the front/turn leg from the down-the-line view, the leg will have some flex in it. Keep in mind that what you see in a golfer's form depends on the view from which you are looking. So in regard to the legs, they look straight from the front view but flexed from the back view – in reality, the knee is truly flexed in *all* dimensions but appears straight from one view.

Position 4 is difficult for most people to get into during their golf swing because they are trying to make the "Turn" too soon. The Turn is the fun part of the golf swing, and it feels powerful – but you need to make the turn a little later than most would think to get the maximum benefit.

To prove my point here, I want you to think someone or something you loved was on the other side of a locked door. They are in imminent danger, and the only way for you to help them is to knock down the door. How would you knock down the door?

Would you hit the door with your hip and shoulder at the same time while your head is moving toward the door? Or would you try to knock down the door using the traditional "golf" way of thinking – starting the downswing from the ground up with your feet, knees, hips, etc.? If you chose the well-known ground-up method, you won't be able to generate enough force to knock the door down ... but you might knock *yourself* out.

Look at the pictures of knocking the door down with the *Fighting Golf* method of coordinating your entire body versus the pictures of a golfer leading with their hips.

Have some fun thinking about knocking a door down and watch your ball get knocked down the fairway!

> "THERE'S ONE SECRET TO HITTING HARD, AND THAT IS TO COMPLETELY DEDICATE YOUR BODY. THAT'S THE DIFFERENCE BETWEEN A MAN GOING FORWARD AND A MAN GOING BACKWARD, NO MATTER HOW BIG HE IS."
> **-RAY LEWIS**

RECOMMENDED: You want to use all your force as you work though the impact area.

NOT RECOMMENDED: It is obvious this body positioning will deliver a feeble blow. However, if you look on ranges, you see lots of swings like this.

SWEEP THE FLOOR

To be a good golfer, you need a good imagination. For this image/drill, I need to set up a story first. Imagine you are at your house in the kitchen, and somehow a glass bowl full of sugar falls on the tile floor and smashes into pieces with sugar going everywhere. Now annoyed, you go to get the broom and the dustpan to clean it up. After reading how to do the drill below, the next time you have to grab the broom to clean something up, you will know you are getting more practice on your golf swing.

In order to have the proper impact position, you want to have your hands leading the clubface as you strike the ball. This is the same motion you make when sweeping.

To get all the sugar and debris into the dustpan, you would put the handle of the broom on a slant closer to the dustpan than the broom head. From there, you would move your hands, keeping the slant of the broom fairly constant and the broom head flush with the ground.

If you let the broom head get past your hands, this would create a bigger mess. You wouldn't think of cleaning up the mess by creating a bigger mess. However, if you think you have to "lift" the ball in the air, this is the *exact* way you would move your club.

When using the broom, you are moving the sugar/debris from the side while keeping the pressure of the broom head on the debris. In golf, we are always hitting the side of the ball in a downward manner.

When looking at the pictures, notice the position of my torso and the effect it has on my hands... something to think about in your own swing. If you want to have a firm front wrist at impact, it helps to have your torso on top of your legs, not leaning back.

It is interesting to compare the similarities of efficiently using a broom and making an efficient strike on the golf ball.

*Notice in the **good motion photos above** how the target hand remains flush and the entire front arm moves toward the target. Also notice how low the broom bristles are to the ground.*

Notice in the poor form pictures that the front wrist has broken down because the broom bristles past the hands. Also notice how the head and torso are hanging back and how high the bristles are off the ground.

FOOTWORK FOR FORCE

Boxers need good footwork and so do golfers — really, *all* athletes need good footwork. In order to use your feet properly and feel how to push off with force through the ball, you have to learn how to get your back hip joint to lead your back knee through impact.

I need you to imagine you are about to go on a boat ride. You have one foot on the boat and one foot on the dock, and you need to push the boat away from the dock.

In order to do this, you use your back foot to push off the dock. When you do that, you will feel the force pushing from your instep and notice that you are directing that energy toward your front leg. Let me show you how to apply this to golf, and what it will look like if you are on the driving range or working on this footwork at home.

When you start your swing at address, your back hip joint is closer to the target than your back knee. The back hip joint will stay in front of your back knee the entire swing, all the way to the finish.

You use your back foot and leg to push yourself and the club through the hitting area. When you start to push off, you will feel yourself rolling to the instep of your back foot. When this happens, you will feel your instep rolling and pressing into the ground while the back half of your foot starts to come off the ground. From there, the heel starts to come off the ground; as you continue to rotate, you end up finishing all the way on tippy toe of the back foot.

When you push off with your back hip leading the knee, you will feel a proper weight shift. And it makes it easier to work through to your front leg easily and to a balanced finish.

When a golfer pushes off with their back leg in such a manner where the knee passes the back hip joint, it causes the hips to twist too soon, resulting in the back shoulder falling and a path that will most likely come from out to in.

The more you can feel your feet in the swing and learn how to push off powerfully the more your ball striking will improve.

Look at the pictures on the next page to figure out the move…it allows you to do all sorts of fun things – hard hip punching (coming up in Position 5), straight shots, and good balance.

CHECKPOINTS — POSITION 4

BODY CHECK
Upper Body
- Target arm and shaft are in a straight line in front of the inside of the target leg.
- Your head is moving toward your front leg.
- Your head is positioned on the same angle as your spine, meaning your nose will be in line with your sternum.
- If there were a stake coming out the logo of your glove on your front hand, it would be parallel to the target line.

Lower Body
- Your zipper is almost on top of the front foot.
- The back foot has rolled to the instep of the foot, with the heel just starting to come off the ground.
- Both knees should still have the same amount of flex as they did at address.
- From the down-the-line view, your back knee should be inside your toe line; if the knee is past the toe line, the golfer is going to have a difficult time finishing in balance.

CLUB CHECK
Clubface
The clubface should be square to the target line.

Club shaft
The club shaft should be traveling down the target line.
The club shaft should be either on a slight forward lean at impact or straight up and down at Position 4.

"A NOVEL IS A COLLISION OF IDEAS. THREE OR FOUR THREADS MAY BE FLOATING AROUND IN THE WRITER'S CONSCIOUSNESS, AND AT A SINGLE MOMENT IN TIME, THESE IDEAS COLLIDE AND PRODUCE A NOVEL."
—ANITA SHREVE

LIKE A NOVEL, YOUR GOLF SWING IS A MENTAL COLLISION OF YOUR SWING THOUGHTS. GIVE YOURSELF TIME TO UNDERSTAND WHAT THOUGHTS FIT TOGETHER LIKE THE PIECES OF A PUZZLE FOR THAT PERFECT SHOT.

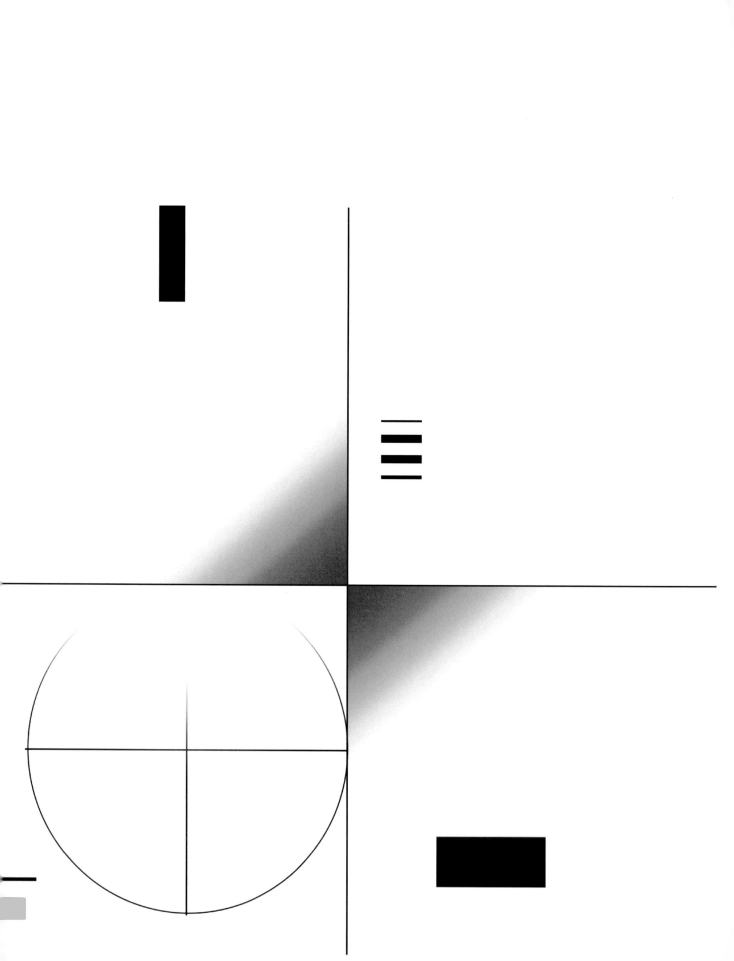

THE SPEED SLOT

POSITION 5 THE SPEED SLOT

Some people think it doesn't matter what happens after you hit the ball because the ball is already gone; however, the part of the swing after you hit the ball is critical when it comes to maximizing your speed, maintaining your balance, and reducing injury.

Think of your swing as consisting of two parts. The first half of the golf swing consists of everything until the moment of impact, and the second half of the swing would be from impact to the finish. If you can stay on plane during the second half of your swing, then you will maximize your speed and also have the ability to maintain your balance. If you get off plane on either side, you have to make a compensation with your body, resulting in a "grind" or "speed leak."

The golf club is moving the fastest from Position 4 to Position 5; this portion of the swing happens so quickly it is hard to tell if you are doing it properly at full speed. Again, in order to master the second half of the swing, it helps to do lots of slow motion drills at home to feel the body motion so you can then start doing the same motion at faster and faster speeds.

As stated earlier, the purpose of each Striking Position is to have your body and club in balance at the same time. Position 5 is no different. Take a look at the picture on the other page. Notice how my body looks easily balanced. I could hold that position for a long period of time and nothing would be hurt or strained.

Largely, Position 5 is just the result of earlier positions in the swing. Practice the drills on the following pages to maximize your Speed Slot.

KNOW HOW
The drills for Position 5 will help you learn how to rotate on plane.

Hip Punch
Bored at a Cocktail Party
Two Handed Shaft Match

THE HIP PUNCH

Boxers use punching bags to work on their skills. I think it would be helpful for golfers to have some punching bags of their own ... we all know that the little white ball gets the best of us sometimes and it would be a good release to hit something!

The goal of this drill is to have you knock out the "punching bag" using your back hip.

You often hear in golf that all the power and the speed in golf swing comes from the hips. There is debate regarding which body part generates the most speed. Keep in mind that, according to Golf the Rabito Way, 76 percent of the speed comes from the hinging and unhinging of the wrists; and 11 percent of the speed comes from the hinging and unhinging of the elbows during the swing. (Carl Rabito and Mike Williams. Golf: The Rabito Way. Orlando: CRM of Orlando, 2013. Electronic book.) Regardless of whether the ultimate speed producer is the hips, the wrists, the elbows, or the earlobes ... if our body is working powerfully and efficiently, we will be maximizing our force and speed.

In my mind, the hips allow for the balance, the direction, and the path of the club. The more our hips work properly, the faster we will be able to turn our chest/core, which in turn whips our wrists and elbows that are the true speed generators ... truly, it is a beautiful blend of energy transfer.

For this drill, pretend you have fists on your hip joints. You also need to imagine that there is a punching bag that is just outside your front leg, even with your hip joints. Your goal is to hit the punching bag as hard as you can with the fist that is attached to the back hip. Once you do this drill a few times with the fists on your hips, you can do the drill with just your back hip.

You will notice a couple of things doing this drill. First, I hope you notice that you have to make a weight transfer onto your front leg to hit the punching bag/ball with full force. If you start twisting your hips without getting all the way on to the front leg, you will barely swipe the ball, and you won't feel powerful.

When you start punching the bag/ball correctly, you will feel how to deliver the maximum force with your lower body while maintaining your balance and reducing the stress in your lower body. You feel what it means when you hear golf instructors say you hit it with your "right side" ... really, they should say *trail* side.

See the pictures on the next page for this drill in action.

Picture 1 - Get into your posture and put fists on your hips.

Picture 2: Loaded to strike.

Picture 3 - The full fury of the back hip has been released through the ball to a balanced finish.

BORED AT A COCKTAIL PARTY

We have all been at cocktail parties that have been a bit dull, and we do different things to keep alert – like shifting our weight from side to side or rocking back and forth on our feet.

In order to do this drill you just need your body. Stand up straight and cross your arms at your chest. (You see this stance all the time.) Make sure your legs are the width they are at posture with your feet flared.

Now I want you to shift your weight so that your head and zipper get closer to your front foot and you feel your hip socket engage. Once you shift your weight so that the bones in your front leg are in a straight line, you will be able to easily turn to a full finish.

If you make a proper weight transfer through the impact area, you will know the bones in your front leg are positioned to where you could stand on one leg. Once you feel like you could stand on one leg, you start to make the turn to the finish. When this move is done properly, you will feel balanced, at your finish, with all your weight on your front foot.

When you finish the bored-at-a-cocktail party move, your upper arms, which are folded, should be level to the ground. The back hip will be directly underneath the back shoulder. This is a balanced position.

If you attempt to twist your hips before the bones on your front leg line up, you will not be able to finish with your body in a straight line and on the toe of your back foot. If you merely twist your hips, you will finish with weight on your back foot, and most likely be on the ball of the back foot and feel out of balance.

See the pictures on the next page. It's pretty easy stuff you do every day. Seriously, I do this when I am waiting in line at the grocery store. For the rest of your life, know where your center of gravity is and where you feel the weight in your feet. It will serve you well!

This drill is great for feeling weight transfer and for noticing how important your head is in allowing the rest of the body to work properly. If the head stays back too long, it prevents the back leg from working properly. Besides, you would look weird leaving your head back and trying to turn at a cocktail party. If you do this drill correctly, no one will notice you are working on your swing.

Of course, making air swings is *completely* normal to all you golfers out there!
Keep moving and keep getting better!

Picture 1: I am standing normally with my arms crossed.

Picture 2: I have transferred all my weight on top my front leg. Notice how I am beginning to push off the back foot.

Picture 3: My entire body has turned to the target. My back hip is under my back shoulder and my front foot is flat on the ground. Also I am on the tippy toe of my back foot.

TWO-HANDED SHAFT MATCH

Position 5 works on staying on plane during the second half of the golf swing. If you do this drill properly, you will feel your lower body working in tandem with the golf club.

For this drill you will need two clubs in succession; for example, a 9-iron and an 8-iron. If you have a starter set, just grab two clubs.

Place one club in each hand and rest both clubheads square on the ground with a ball sandwiched between the two clubheads. Now imagine you are making a "butterfly" move and take each club away until the golf clubs are parallel to the ground and you feel like the toe of each clubhead is tilted slightly back toward the back wall if you are practicing indoors.

Once the clubs are parallel to the ground, move the back half of your body and the club in your trail hand to touch the "target side" club while touching the ball at the bottom of the arc. You must stay on plane to match the shaft in your target hand.

This drill also gives you an idea of how the hands release. The club moves quickly through the swing; however, the clubface is gradually and continuously moving. Some golfers think they have to "roll" their hands quickly through impact. Due to the way the clubhead is weighted, if your body is moving properly, the turning of the body should help create the needed rotation to square the clubface.

Do this drill a few times and notice what happens with your body and the clubface. You will notice how they start to work in tandem.

SWING PLANE IS DIFFICULT IS BECAUSE IT IS INVISIBLE WHEN YOU ARE SWINGING. YOU HAVE TO IMAGINE IT IN YOUR MIND'S EYE. IF YOU DON'T UNDERSTAND SWING PLANE, THEN YOU DON'T EVEN KNOW WHAT TO IMAGINE.

Let this drill be your guide to seeing what swing plane looks and feels like when the shaft is parallel to the ground in the downswing to the through swing.

Remember: Take care of the straight lines, and the curves will take care of themselves.

CHECKPOINTS — POSITION 5

BODY CHECK
Upper Body
- Your eyes are parallel to the ground with your eyes looking down the fairway.
- Your nose, sternum, and belly button are facing down the fairway.

Lower Body
- Your back hip is flush with an imaginary wall. (see picture)
- Your back hip is directly below your back shoulder.
- You should be balanced, and a line should be able to be drawn through your shoulder, to your hip, to your knee.
- You are on the toe of the back foot.

CLUB CHECK
Clubface
The clubface is on plane with the toe of the club facing toward the "back wall."

Club Shaft
The club shaft is parallel to ground and parallel to the target line.

At Position 5, you should feel completely in balance on your front side at this point in your swing.

Your nose, sternum, belly button, club, and the shoe laces on your back shoe will all be facing down the fairway at this point.

BALANCE IS POWER AND FLUIDITY CREATES SPEED!

POSITION 6

WALL WORTHY

KNOWLEDGE

POSITION 6 WALL WORTHY

You want a "picture-perfect," balanced, polished finish; you never want to look like you are going to fall over or are in some sort of contortion. With the ideal finish pose, you should be proud to display a photograph of it on your office wall or on social media.

The neat thing about the golf swing is that it is just a series of chain reactions. If you have mastered positions 1-5, Position 6 is almost a given.

When watching your swing on camera, from the down-the-line view, you want the shaft to exit through your target shoulder if it is staying on plane. If the shaft is exiting through your ribcage, the shaft is under plane and will rob you of some speed.

The finish is an interesting position. All golfers know where they would *like* to be at the finish. However, the problem is that most golfers fake their finish! You goal should be able to swing as quickly as you want and finish "cleanly" in balance.

Keep reading, and let's see if we can polish the last piece of your swing and get your finish "wall worthy."

"THE HARDEST PART ABOUT FINISHING IS STARTING."
—JAROD KINTZ

This quote absolutely applies to your quest to master your golf swing. Your finish is simply the result of your earlier movements. It will tell you if you did the other movements correctly. The better you get at Position 1, the better you will be at Position 6.

There is no need to obsess on your finish since it is a result. Obsess on your grip, posture, and the start of your swing; on the downswing, be the golf ball assassin. Good Luck!

THE GOLF EXCHANGE

Boxers train using exchanges by combining punches like the jab, the uppercut, and the cross. For this golfing move we are going to make up our own movement, or Golf Exchange, called **Pull Back, Golf Uppercut**

Set up in your golf posture and put up your dukes by bending your elbows and making fists with both hands. When you put up your dukes, make sure you are on your Golfing Tilt. From here I want you to do a "Golf Exchange."

There are two parts to this Golf Exchange:
Part 1 – Pull Back: With your dukes up, pull back with your back shoulder like you're going to throw a punch or elbow someone behind you.
Part 2 – Golf Uppercut: Circle your back fist downward below your belt, and then back up to hit a punching bag that is outside and above your front foot.

Look at the pictures below and on the next page and mimic the motions to feel what it will be like to glide into a good finish position.

In golf, just like fighting, you have to be able to move quickly, change directions and keep your feet underneath you.

Pictures of the GOLF UPPERCUT portion of the Golf Exchange with a fist and with a club.

PUTTING IT ALL TOGETHER

Training **Fighting Golf** principles into your game.

Conceptually
- Reread the chapters on the Grip and the Power Platform to know how to position your bones.
- Visualize making all the motions described and envision doing the drills as you sit and read the book.
- Always keep in mind the positioning of your body, the straight lines in the golf swing, and the balance points of the golf club.

In Motion Application
- Practice "learning speed," which is the rate of speed where you *know* where your body and club are during the swing.
- Practice with your eyes closed.
- Get a lot of reps. Many golfers complain that they just don't have enough time to hit enough balls to get better. Fighting Golf has solved that for you too!
  - The Impact Improver is truly golf's punching bag. With a specially designed Strike Shield™ that adheres to your own club, you can practice indoors because the provided Impact Balls stick to the Strike Shield when the ball is struck. It allows you train whenever you like, wherever you like, and with as many strikes as you like - without putting any holes in the wall.

THANK YOU FOR READING THIS BOOK!

I hope you enjoyed Fighting Golf and came away with some mental nuggets that can help you with your game.

I want you to be a warrior in heart and mind with the club as your weapon. Always be in position to *deliver* a blow instead of a position where *you* could be knocked out.

My advice to you: Have fun, glide through your swing while Wielding the Weight, and Knock Out a great round of golf.

See you on the range … and always Flow with Force & Fly!
Tiffany

FIGHTING GOLF is about the art of movement, and all of that starts in the mind. Few understood the mind and the movement like Bruce Lee: legendary martial artist, actor, and philosopher. His quotes below show the mindset of success weaves through fighting, golf, and life.

"Obey the principles without being bound by them."

"A quick temper will make a fool of you soon enough."

"The possession of anything begins in the mind."

"Take things as they are. Punch when you have to punch.
Kick when you have to kick."

"Absorb what is useful, discard what is useless
and add what is specifically your own."

"Do not allow negative thoughts to enter your mind
for they are the weeds that strangle confidence."

"I fear not the man who has practiced 10,000 kicks once,
but I fear the man who had practiced one kick 10,000 times."

"Choose the positive. You have choice, you are master of your attitude,
choose the positive, the constructive. Optimism is a faith that leads to success."

In my mind this last quote from Bruce Lee is the essence of Fighting Golf.

**"Do not be tense, just be ready, not thinking but not dreaming,
not being set but being flexible. It is being "wholly" and quietly alive,
aware and alert, ready for whatever may come."**

ENJOY THE GAME – ENJOY YOUR LIFE – FLOW WITH FORCE & FLY!

THE END

This is the end of this book and the
beginning of your journey to be the
best Fighting Golfer you can become.

Now you will have me, my trusted colleagues, and the
Fighting Golf Philosophy in *your* corner!

If you would like more information to maximize
your learning, development, and mastery
of your game please go to

www.FightingGolf.com

ABOUT THE AUTHOR

Regarded as one of the most effective and sought-after instructors in the Northeast, Tiffany Faucette brings a wealth of experience to her students at all playing levels via targeted teaching. She knows how to connect mentally with a student to get them to improve their swing motion. She firmly believes in both working hard and having fun, in practice and on the course.

A native of Ormond Beach, FL, Faucette took up the game of golf at age 17 and went on to play for and captain the Florida State University women's team while earning a degree in business. After winning numerous amateur accolades, including 1997's Titleist/Golfweek top-ranked amateur, Faucette spent the next 11 years competing professionally. She competed in two majors: the U.S. Women's Open and the McDonald's LPGA Championship—and in every major women's tour including the LPGA Futures, Asian, European and Canadian Tours.

Faucette brings her impressive background and stats to her true passion: teaching players at all levels to love and improve her game. She has been recognized for her teaching by the LPGA—Teacher of the Year NE, Golf Range Association of America Top 50, LPGA Global Education Team, and U.S. Kids Golf Top 50, Best in Loudoun, among others. In addition to working directly with students, Faucette brings her experience and motivational tips to audiences, speaking both to athletes and the general public in seminars about teaching, the biomechanics of the game, and making positive changes to help achieve life goals.

Presently, Faucette is the Lead Instructor at 1757 Golf Club, Ashburn, VA. In addition to her heavy teaching schedule, she is actively developing and marketing a variety of instructional tools—including innovative products and manuals—to bring her expertise to all players looking to "punish that little white ball." Learn more about Tiffany Faucette at www.fightinggolf.com.